T0318252

# The Epistemology and Morality of Human Kinds

Natural kinds is a widely used and pivotal concept in philosophy – the idea being that the classifications and taxonomies employed by science correspond to the real kinds in nature. Natural kinds are often opposed to the idea of kinds in the human and social sciences, which are typically seen as social constructions, characterised by changing norms and resisting scientific reduction. Yet human beings are also a subject of scientific study. Does this mean humans fall into corresponding kinds of their own?

In *The Epistemology and Morality of Human Kinds* Marion Godman defends the idea of human kinds. She first examines the scientific use and nature of human kinds, considering the arguments of key philosophers whose work bears upon human kinds, such as Ian Hacking, John Searle, Richard Boyd and Ruth Millikan. Using the examples of gender, ethnic minorities and Buddhism she then argues that human kinds are a result of ongoing historical reproduction, chiefly due to pre-existing cultural models and social learning. Her novel argument shifts the focus away from the reductionism characteristic of research about human kinds. Instead, she argues that they are "multiply projectable" and deserving of scientific study not in spite of, but because of their role in explaining our identity, injustice and the emergence of group rights.

**Marion Godman** is an Assistant Professor in the Department of Political Science at Aarhus University, Denmark and an Affiliated Scholar of the History and Philosophy of Science Department at Cambridge University, UK. She is currently a recipient of a Sapere Aude research leader grant examining what a theory of human kinds (or groups) can tell us about the basis for group rights.

# Routledge Focus on Philosophy

*Routledge Focus on Philosophy* is an exciting and innovative new series, capturing and disseminating some of the best and most exciting new research in philosophy in short book form. Peer reviewed and at a maximum of fifty thousand words shorter than the typical research monograph, *Routledge Focus on Philosophy* titles are available in both ebook and print on demand format. Tackling big topics in a digestible format the series opens up important philosophical research for a wider audience, and as such is invaluable reading for the scholar, researcher and student seeking to keep their finger on the pulse of the discipline. The series also reflects the growing interdisciplinarity within philosophy and will be of interest to those in related disciplines across the humanities and social sciences.

**The Repugnant Conclusion**
A Philosophical Inquiry
*Christopher Cowie*

**Confucianism and the Philosophy of Well-Being**
*Richard Kim*

**Neurofunctional Prudence and Morality**
A Philosophical Theory
*Marcus Arvan*

**The Epistemology and Morality of Human Kinds**
*Marion Godman*

**A Defence of Nihilism**
*James Tartaglia and Tracy Llanera*

For more information about this series, please visit: www.routledge.com/ Routledge-Focus-on-Philosophy/book-series/RFP

# The Epistemology and Morality of Human Kinds

**Marion Godman**

Routledge
Taylor & Francis Group
LONDON AND NEW YORK

First published 2021
by Routledge
2 Park Square, Milton Park, Abingdon, Oxon OX14 4RN

and by Routledge
605 Third Avenue, New York, NY 10017

*Routledge is an imprint of the Taylor & Francis Group, an informa business*

Copyright © 2021 Marion Godman

*British Library Cataloguing-in-Publication Data*
A catalogue record for this book is available from the British Library

*Library of Congress Cataloging-in-Publication Data*
Names: Godman, Marion, author.
Title: The epistemology and morality of human kinds / Marion Godman.
Description: Abingdon, Oxon ; New York, NY : Routledge, 2021. |
 Series: Routledge focus on philosophy | Includes bibliographical
 references and index.
Identifiers: LCCN 2020031491 | ISBN 9781138724303 (hbk) |
 ISBN 9781315190082 (ebk)
Subjects: LCSH: Human beings—Philosophy. | Social epistemology. |
 Sociobiology.
Classification: LCC BD450 .G587 2021 | DDC 128—dc23
LC record available at https://lccn.loc.gov/2020031491

ISBN 13: 978-1-138-72430-3 (hbk)
ISBN 13: 978-0-367-65318-7 (pbk)

Typeset in Times New Roman
by Apex CoVantage, LLC

*For my Grannie, Mary Fallis*

# Contents

*Acknowledgments*                                                           viii

1   Introduction                                                              1

2   Human kinds for knowledge and as levers for change                       5

3   Existing approaches to human kinds                                       21

4   Historical kinds                                                         45

5   Gender as a historical kind: a plea for reclassification                 58

6   What is culture and how is it realized?                                  70

7   How historical kinds achieve a moral standing                           78

8   Conclusion: the key contributions of human
    historical kinds                                                         97

    *Bibliography*                                                          101
    *Index*                                                                 110

# Acknowledgments

The bulk of this book was written when I found myself between temporary research contracts and had little funding or institutional support to lean on. I am therefore especially indebted to many individuals who have supported me during this time, ensuring that the book came to fruition.

First, I am indebted to a category of individuals that I am fortunate to consider both my friends and my colleagues. Many have read and commented on drafts of different parts of the book; all have offered crucial encouragement and ideas that made me feel that this book was worth writing. Thank you, Anna Alexandova, Paloma Atencia, Martin Bellander, Olle Blomberg, Sofia Bull, Ophelia Deroy, Luis Mireles Flores, Cecilia Hansson, Elselijn Kingma, Ivana Konvalinka, Jaakko Kuorikoski, Simo Kyllönen, Sonja LaBianca, Pekka Mäkelä, Magda Malecka, Paolo Mantovani, Michiru Nagatsu, Samuli Reijula, Mikko Salmela, Sanna Tirkkonen, Pilvi Toppinen, Thomas Szanto, Ville Paukkonen, Moises Vaca, and Julie Zahle. In this category I owe a special thank you to Anneli Jefferson for "galloping through the book in breakneck speed" and still making loads of sense, and to Caterina Marchionni, from whom I gain so many laughs, ideas and comfort.

Drafts of Chapters 1, 2 and 3 have been presented at two "brown bag seminars" hosted by the TINT Centre of Philosophy of Social Science at Helsinki University, where I received excellent comments from the audience. For reading drafts of what have since become Chapters 4, 5 and 6, I am grateful to Olivier Lemiere. And with respect to Chapter 7, I wish to thank a brilliant group of Danish philosophers – Thor Grünbaum, Alexander Heape, Nils Holtug, Kasper Lippert-Rasmussen and Maria Kjær Rasmussen – for discussions.

The importance of the past decade's conversations that I have had with David Papineau is hard to underestimate. Thank you, David, for your unwavering support and always exciting collaborations. As no one could miss reading this book, I am immensely grateful to Ruth Millikan for enduring philosophical inspiration. I also wish to thank Tim Lewens and Klemens Kappel for supporting my affiliations with Cambridge and Copenhagen Universities, respectively, at a crucial time.

To be frank, this book would also not have been possible without the Nordic welfare states system of unemployment insurance that has filled a gap in salary and funding. I am currently a happy recipient of research grants from the Danish Research Council (Sagsnummer: 9062-00049B) for the foreseeable future. Thanks to the council and to Kasper Lippert-Rasmussen for including me in a new and exciting research center for the study of discrimination at Aarhus University. I would also like to thank my editors at Routledge, Tony Bruce and Adam Johnson, for their patience with this book's completion, and the anonymous referees for their constructive and dedicated feedback that made the book much better.

To our daughter, Frances Irja, born during the time of writing this book: thank you for taking long naps at crucial junctions and for just being such a joy when you wake up. And tack and kiitos Petri for sharing the joy with me and for giving me the space to be absorbed in writing. Speaking of space for writing, a warm thanks also to Renia, Natasha and others at Frances' daycare, Vandverket.

Finally, to my mom Luella, brothers Robert and Brent, sister Nicola, and bosom friends Sara, Caterina, Kate, Lina and Josefine: whatever would I do without you!

This book is dedicated to my Grannie, Mary. The reasons why role models matter should be clear in this book. She has and continues to be a role model to me.

*Copenhagen, June 19, 2020*

As a thirteen-year-old, I found myself in a clearing in a wood outside of Moscow, at a secret – one might say underground, though it was out in the open – gathering of Jewish cultural activists. People went up in front of the crowd, one, two, or several at a time, with guitars and without, and sang from a limited repertoire of Hebrew and Yiddish songs. That is, they sang the same three or four songs over and over. The tunes scraped something inside of me, making an organ I didn't know I had – located just above the breastbone – tingle with a sense of belonging. I was surrounded by strangers, sitting, as we were, on logs laid across the grass, and I remember their faces to this day. I looked at them and thought, *This is who I am.* The "this" in this was "Jewish". From my perch thirty-seven years later, I'd add "in a secular cultural community" and "in the Soviet Union", but back then space was too small to require elaboration. Everything about it seemed self-evident – once I knew what I was, I would just be it. In fact, the people in front of me, singing those songs, were trying to figure out how to be Jewish in a country that had erased Jewishness. Now I'd like to think that it was watching people learning to inhabit an identity that made me tingle.

Masha Gessen, *To be or not to be*, 2018 (*The New Yorker*)

# 1 Introduction

We humans are very ambivalent about the categorization of ourselves and others. Our categorizing into kinds of people – kinds of gender, and kinds of religion, for example – seems important for understanding the world, and it also seems crucial to our self-understanding and for our identity. At the same time, we are reluctant to categorize as it appears associated with practices of exclusion, stereotypes and misguided generalizations.

I remember this ambivalence from my early schooldays. I had a Canadian mother who spoke a different language and who, in contrast to the other Swedish moms, was never afraid to volunteer her opinions at parent-school meetings at our Swedish rural school. This was my sense of not belonging to the same category as my peers. At the same time, I was aware I was not *as* different as the Colombian boy at school. Moreover, I also took comfort in being different. Being Canadian became an explanation of the difference, and it was a source of secret pride. One of my friends tells me about his daughters who are Japanese-Estonian living in Finland and how they navigate between the different categories they belong to. They are fine to be picked up by their parents at school and at ease with their friends hearing them speak both Japanese and Estonian. It is when their grandmother shows up speaking Russian that they get embarrassed and ask their parents to pick them up instead.

This book is about these human kinds themselves, such as being Canadian or being a girl. Can this seemingly inescapable use of human categories be explained by something prior to their use, something outside our psychological disposition to categorize? And, what sort of knowledge can we hope to attain from these kinds? Finally, how can this knowledge be put to use in policies combating injustices, some of which we begin to fathom already in childhood? I hope to address these central questions in the course of this book.

I will suggest that many human kinds are historical kinds. They are historical kinds because any common tendencies among their members is achieved through chains of reproduction, or lineages, to common models. The past decades of work on cultural evolution has taught us about how humans reproduce not only their genetic material, but also a range of behavior, language, skills and knowledge through social learning and through a pre-existing culture. Much of this *cultural reproduction* is only channeled among certain groups of individuals: groups which I will argue belong to kinds of a certain gender, ethnicity or ideology. Human *historical* kinds thus come about due to chains of reproduction that only exist between certain groups of individuals within a particular culture. Our biology also plays a role, but it sits in the backseat for the kinds I will discuss where culture is queen.

In building my account, it will be evident how very much indebted I am to Ruth Millikan's account of both real kinds and historical kinds (1999, 2000, 2017). But our views also differ both in terms of focus[1] and substance. Some specific differences will be discussed in Chapters 5 and 6, but I should note the main difference from the outset. In the paper "Historical kinds and the 'special sciences'", Millikan dismisses much of the scientific importance of historical kinds by saying that: "[R]elatively few [historical kinds] have numerous and interesting properties in common, or have these with high regularity" (1999, p. 56). With respect to having "interesting properties" in common, I disagree with her outright, and hopefully my different cases of human kinds in Chapters 4–7 can convince you of just how interesting properties of historical kinds can be. With respect to the criteria of having "numerous" properties in common and of "high regularity", I think these criteria are both too demanding and unnecessary for kindhood – especially in the human sciences. In the next chapter I will show why the criteria are unnecessary, adding my own criteria for kindhood.

So, in contrast to Millikan, it is my firm belief that human *historical* kinds also have a crucial and interesting scientific and moral role to play. Indeed, it is the aim of this book to demonstrate this point. I believe it is an important job, especially in a world that is increasingly skeptical of science in general and not least when it comes to the human sciences and its categories.

This brings me to the question of readership. As my discussion concerns a range of cases and tries to find a synthesis among materials from many fields – including evolutionary biology, anthropology, history, gender studies and developmental and social psychology – I would hope it appeals to a broad range of students and researchers. That said, this is a research monograph in philosophy, and not all I will say will be interesting or relevant to everyone, so I will give a brief roadmap of the book that indicates the readership I have in mind for each chapter.[2]

The next chapter (2) is intended to motivate the philosophical talk about natural kinds and human kinds. I argue that we need a notion of kinds to make robust knowledge claims in the human sciences, even if – or rather *especially if* – one wishes to resist the generalizations and categorizations associated with supposed kinds. My discussion focuses on key philosophy of science concepts such as *induction, generalizations and common causes*. I also touch on the issue of essentialism and the psychological and political debates surrounding the categorization of human kinds. My hope is that this discussion will both introduce the key issues for the following chapters and be accessible to a broad audience looking to have a sense of what all the philosophical fuss about kinds and human kinds is about.

Chapter 3 critically discusses popular alternative approaches to human kinds and identifies useful lessons from each approach. The accounts discussed are multiple realization, functionalism, social ontology, looping effects, homeostatic mechanisms and social construction. This chapter will probably mostly be interesting to philosophers who are more specialized on human kinds and who are curious about the discussion more broadly. Other readers can safely skip ahead.

Chapter 4 lays out the basics of my position about human kinds as historical kinds. It describes what historical kinds are and how we can explain them using the common-cause framework outlined in Chapter 2. This chapter really has two parts in terms of audience. For a general audience to get the basic idea of what historical kinds are, one may get away with reading only the relatively short beginning of Chapter 4 (Historical kinds), but if one wants some more arguments, for the position, I encourage general readers to also read Sections 4.1 (Lineages as common-cause explanations) and 4.2 (Humankind and Swampkinds: how lineages individuate).

The following Chapters 5–7, are all organized around particular case studies of human kinds as historical kinds. They will probably attract readers according to their interests in the particular cases, but also depending on what aspect of historical kinds one is interested in. My historical-reproductive account of human kinds raises an obvious issue of scope: how many human kinds are *historical* human kinds? Heads up that I will probably disappoint some readers by not directly answering this question. Instead, my argument will be on a case-by-case basis in Chapters 4–7.

Chapter 5 is on gender and how (re)classification according to cultural lineages helps us better demarcate our kinds of gender and resulting generalizations. Chapter 6 is about cultural kinds more broadly, which are not necessarily kinds of people, such as different religions and ideologies. I describe some principles that allow us to *organize* our knowledge based on such kinds to assist the identification of new kinds and novel properties. Chapter 7 discusses the particularly contentious cases of race and ethnicity from the purview of the Nordic north and the racial hygiene studies early of the 20th century. I argue that cases such as these demonstrate how some historical kinds, of say ethnicity and gender, may acquire a certain moral standing and give rise to group rights.

Those most interested in the *moral and political* role of human kinds should focus on Sections 2.4 (Human kinds as levers of social change), 3.2 (Human kinds as social institutions) and Chapter 7 (How historical kinds achieve a moral standing). I believe these parts of the book can also mostly be read independently of the other parts (perhaps assisted by the key section on historical kinds at the beginning of Chapter 4 and in the final summary (Chapter 8)).

Finally, to assist readers interested in the overall argument, I have tried to include summaries of each chapter's arguments either at the beginning or end of each chapter. The conclusion tries to summarize the main claims of the book and references the part of the book in which the arguments for the claims are made. Now, let's get to work.

## Notes

1 Millikan's work on real kinds, where historical kinds are a subcategory, is mostly concerned with presenting a view about our language and psychology of certain concepts – what she has called *substance concepts* (2000) and later, *unicepts* (2017). I also give much more space to exploring the possibility that many *human kinds* are historical kinds than she has done in her work.

2 I fear I may already have frightened some readers as the term "human kinds" is a somewhat awkward technical term that has grown out of discussions about natural kinds in academic philosophy. At some points of my discussion, it might be easy enough to supplement with the more colloquial term "human group" but, for reasons that will become clear in Chapter 2, for the most part, we need to retain "kind" as a specific term of art.

# 2 Human kinds for knowledge and as levers for change

Human beings are grouped into kinds in the human and life sciences, but also in policy. Indeed, we use concepts like "women", "Canadian" and "farmer" as a central part of our everyday conversation and learning.[1] But the very ubiquity of these concepts and their unstable usage prompts the following question: how is it that we can have a *science*, bodies of reliable empirical knowledge about humans – knowledge which can also be produced outside academia (such as within think tanks, policy-making bodies and journalism) – that is not mere conjecture or a hunch? This concern about justifying knowledge in the human sciences is also at the forefront in public discourse. A common complaint, leveled at social sciences, gender studies and anthropology alike, is that they are not *scientific* enough (compared to biochemistry, for example).

To deal with this concern, I will argue we must find a way of backing up the *empirical generalizations* found in these bodies of knowledge. This will, in turn, require backing up the *kinds* upon which these generalizations rest. But before we get ahead of ourselves, we may want to have a closer look at what type of knowledge is in question.

## 2.1 Knowledge in the human sciences: generalizations, comparisons and generics

Here are two features (or at least, aims) of the scientific knowledge regarded as gold standard: knowledge that is *strict and lawful* and generalizations that are *universally applicable*.[2] With the possible exception of some economists, I think there is also a general consensus that using this model of knowledge in the human sciences just will not do.

First, reliable generalizations are undoubtedly to be aimed at, but they are barely lawlike, much less constitute actual laws. Indeed, one common definition of generalizations in the human and "special" sciences is that they are *ceteris paribus*, i.e. they hold with exceptions (Fodor, 1974). As for the criterion that the generalizations should be *universally* applicable, this simply does not make much sense in the human sciences. Any knowledge that is applicable to some or most human beings should clearly not be applicable to chairs, reindeer or blocks of granite. Such knowledge is applicable specifically to *all* or *a certain range* of humans or *a range* of products of human activities.

That said, in making knowledge claims, it is also important to be careful about the precise *scope* of one's generalizations. Consider the notion of a "case study". The interest in such studies arguably lies in their potential to serve as a general model for other cases, but the scope will often need to be made explicit in order to be precisely a *case* study. The importance of being clear about one's scope is a theme we will have reason to return to.

Clearly, we need a different standard to judge the body of empirical knowledge in the human sciences. While it is not strict, lawful or universal, this knowledge, arguably like all knowledge, does involve claims of generalizability. It is the empirical generalizations that the human sciences may sometimes acquire through experimentation, but more often through general observation, correlation and statistical inference.

Take, for example, the following sample of empirical generalizations that purport to be true factual statements in the human sciences: "*Young women* are more likely to go bust than are *young men*"; "*Doctors* have the highest rate of suicide of any professional group"; "*Transgender students* have a relatively higher risk of victimization".[3] These are claims about (young) women, (young) men, medical doctors and transgender students. The results are hardly important because they constitute scientific laws (they may not be lawlike at all). I suggest they are significant because they constitute a basis for generating broader knowledge about certain groups and certain individuals. This in turn can lead to policy interventions such as providing subsidies for young women starting their own businesses, implementing structural workplace reforms that allow doctors to cope with their work-related stress and introducing measures that specifically benefit transgender individuals on college campuses.

A couple of things about these groups and the generalizations are not apparent in typical talk about inductive inferences and quantifications. The first is that the range of generalizations that ought to concern us is not limited to tendencies *within* certain human groups, but also generalizations that have to do with the variance that exists *between groups*. This is highly typical in the case of sex and gender categories.[4] Here the emphasis is not on how members of a group F are similar according to some characteristic $C_1$, it is on how common $C_1$ in this one group, F, is in *comparison* with how common $C_1$ is within another group, M. In what follows I refer to this scientific inference as *comparative tendency*, thereby indicating that the tendency within a group is chiefly, and perhaps only, relative to a certain comparison.

Claims about comparative tendency among group members show just how weak the notion of generalization is in the human sciences. Indeed, the notion of comparative tendency works for generalizations that are not even indicative of a general tendency within a group. For example, doctors may be relatively more likely to commit suicide than any other professional group, but, fortunately, it is also known that the majority of doctors do not commit suicide.[5]

At this point, one might ask to what extent these statements even count as generalizations at all. Shouldn't the human sciences at least aim at quantifiable or statistically secured generalizations that indicate exactly how representative a property is of a particular group ("*80 percent of* women are F"), or at least give a rough approximation ("*Most* men are E" and "*Only some* girls are G")?

However, many general/kind terms function in *generic statements*. In such statements, properties are ascribed to groups and individuals by means of *unquantified* generalizations such as "Women are F", "Typically men like to E" and "Generally G belongs to girls". Generics are also very puzzling, as Sarah-Jane Leslie (2008) has drawn to our attention. Generics seem to point to the truth even if there are plenty of exceptions – in fact, even if the vast majority of instances of a group are exceptions to the generalization. This seems true for the doctor and transgender student examples, for instance. Consider also two of Leslie's non-human kind examples (2008, p. 13ff.): "Sharks attack bathers" and "Mosquitoes carry the West Nile virus". In actual fact, most sharks do not attack bathers and most mosquitoes do not carry the West Nile virus. All the same, the generics seem to indicate the truth.[6]

One might think that the prevalence of generics just bolsters the idea that prejudice and stereotypes inevitably infiltrate the use of human categories – especially when applied in unquantified ways. I think this is too hasty. Although quantification concerning the extent to which the property is representative of a group is probably advisable in many cases, such measures might not always be obtainable due to small sample sizes or other methodological constraints. Moreover, when we form hypotheses, it seems one must inevitably start with generics that posit some hypothetical, often comparative, tendency within groups. In fact, once one acknowledges the morally justified reasons for studying between- and within-group similarities, which I will argue for in a moment, one has an independent reason for stating matters as generics when quantification is not possible or feasible.

Still, if it were only for the weak notion of comparative tendency between groups, one might think the human sciences were, at least in the long run, doomed. Fortunately, however, what these categories lack in terms of strength and regularity, I suggest they might make up in terms of what might be called "multiple projectability" or in supporting multiple comparative tendencies. This is also where the concept of kinds enters our story.

## 2.2   Horse vs. White horse: kinds support *many, many* generalizations

Many human categories are distinguished by the fact that their instances have many, many properties in common to be investigated. John Stuart Mill used the term "kind" to capture such categories:

> By a kind, it will be remembered, we mean one of those classes which are distinguished from all others not by one or a few definite properties, but by an unknown multitude of them. The class horse is a kind, because the things which agree in possessing the characters by which we recognize a horse, agree in a great number of properties, as we know, and, it cannot be doubted, in a great many more than we know.
>
> ([1886]1974, Ch 6, § 4, pp. 703–704)

Here Mill draws attention to the value of groups that form kinds to the inductive sciences. Horses may not be alike in all respects – they vary in size, color and many other features – but they are alike in having manes, tails, a liking for hay and many other anatomical and behavioral features. In short, there are many true instances of the schema, *All horses are F*. There simply is much to learn about horses as a category.

It is worth noting how this Millian conception of kinds contrasts with what is now quite pervasive talk of *natural kind properties* of individuals (e.g. Armstrong, 1980) or indeed of *social categories* as *properties* of individual human beings (e.g. Sveinsdóttir, 2013).[7] If being a member of a kind means being a bearer of *multiple* properties, then it follows that natural kinds are actually *not* akin to properties. It is true that kind terms may function as both subjects (A *dog* has fur) and predicates (Conan is a *dog*), but the fact that kind terms can be used as predicates (Conan is a *dog*) does not show that kinds are properties. Instead, the primary function of a kind is to be the *bearer of properties* (and is not a property in itself). It follows that the primary epistemic and linguistic role of kind terms is being a *subject* for predication (for a more detailed discussion, see Millikan, 2000, 2017).

For Mill, however, mere richness, in sharing multiple features, is not the main point: it must also be *open-ended* in that instances have the potential to share properties of which one may as yet be ignorant. Millikan seems to share this view (1999, p. 56). I do not want to commit to the idea that there is an *unlimited* number of things that we can learn about each kind. The exact number of generalizations will probably vary among different kinds, but there has to be more than a couple. The same goes for their reliability. Not all kinds are born equal in terms of inferential reliability or fecundity. But we should not get too hung up on the quantity and reliability of generalizations, since the important message in Mill's account of kinds – and one that we should accept – is that there are more valid generalizations of the kind's instances than those that are *immediately obvious*.

For some categories, this is clearly not the case. Mill, for example, distinguishes a category such as *Horse* from the category *White horse*:

> [W]hite horse, therefore, is not a kind; because horses which agree in whiteness do not agree in anything else, except the qualities that are common for all horses, and whatever may be the causes or effects of that particular color.
>
> ([1886]1974, Ch 6, § 4, pp. 703–704)

The problem with using a category like *White horse* has nothing to do with the reliability of its whiteness; the instances agree perfectly in that respect. It is rather that there is nothing *new* to learn about white horses that is not already common to all horses. Everything to be learned about white horses logically follows from their being white and from what can be learned about horses in general. It is the category *Horse* that we should be after.

For this reason, a category such as *White horse* adds nothing to our power to anticipate properties. Given that it is necessary first to check that something has the property of being white and is a horse, which are already entailed by the definition of *White horse*, the category cannot function as a means of predicting further unchecked properties. Such categories can never reveal something that is not already known.

This is not the case with genuine kinds. One can typically ascertain kind membership and use the kind to predict properties *without* first checking whether all the anticipated properties are in fact present.[8] Inferences about horses work like this. If we encounter a horse and know that horses have a strong fight-or-flight response, an excellent sense of balance and can sleep both lying down and standing up, then we can assume that this holds for the horse we have just met. We can do this without actually checking that it is the case in each member of the kind.

Other biological species follow the same principle, and species are by no means the only Millian kinds.[9] Higher taxa (*genus, family, order, class, phylum*) also have members that share many features. Thus, all members of the class *Mammalia* have hair, a neocortex, mammary glands, are warm-blooded, and so on. (Note how the features shared by all individual members of some such higher taxon will always be a subset of the features shared by all individual members of any subordinate lower taxon: the features shared by all mammals are a subset of the features shared by all horses, for example.)

Chemical substances display the same structure. All samples of copper share the same density, melting point, electrical and heat conductivity, disposition to combine with other substances and other qualities. Astronomical objects also fall into kinds. All main-sequence stars share a wide range of properties with each other, as do red giants, white dwarfs, supernovae, comets and planets.

So, what about *human* kinds? Can one really be assured that categories of gender and race can be modeled on Mill's kinds with multiple projectable properties among members? Or are they more akin to categories like *White horse*?[10] In fact, when it comes to the category of race, the comparison with white horses is a bit too close for comfort – after all, is race not simply a grouping of individuals who have nothing else in common other than the color of their skin and what is already included in the more general "human" category (see e.g. Gannett, 2010)?

Indeed, the category of race does highlight the lack of clarity regarding intuitions about which, if any, categories in the human sciences could count as Millian kinds where there are lots of generalizations to be had and where the power of anticipation is licensed. But since the category "race" also invites the most controversial epistemic and political questions about human categorization, we need to clear up several further things about human kinds before returning to it in Chapter 7 of this book.

The moral of this section has been to give a first desideratum of what scientifically useful kinds in the human sciences could be; that is, ones that *support multiple empirical generalizations and projections among their members*.

## 2.3   Kinds and common-cause explanations

Perhaps there is a *reason* why *Horse* as a category is preferable to *White horse*. We have seen that generalizations based on the former allow anticipation in ways in which the latter cannot: kinds are in effect rich complexes of correlations. All the many properties characteristic of a kind Horse are *correlated* with each other. Why is that? After all, the different correlated features do not seem to cause each other. The melting point of gold does not cause its density. The bladders of horses do not cause their ears.

It seems a kind has its correlations of properties for some *other* reason. In short, *it is no accident that* different properties are correlated with one another in a kind (Millikan, 2000, p. 18). It is also *no accident* that kinds support multiple empirical generalizations over instances. But this impression of non-accidentality should be probed by asking questions like: why do the properties of a kind come together in the way that they do? What accounts for the correlations of properties exhibited by Cs? What is it about Cs that account for their multifarious resemblance?

Since Aristotle, a tradition claims that essential properties are the properties that uniquely answer these questions and explain the property correlations of kinds (Kung, 1977).[11] Recently, Michael Devitt has argued for a revival of biological essentialism of species along these lines. In his view, empirical generalizations about biological kinds, like the morphology, physiology and behavior across members of a species, demand an explanation: "Why are they so?" and he thinks the intrinsic essential properties of members is the answer (2008, p. 352). Indeed, I have also argued for a kind of essentialism of sorts, namely *historical* essentialism (Godman, 2018a; Godman & Papineau, 2020; Godman, Mallozzi, & Papineau, 2020).

But in the present context, I am concerned that the evocation of essences carries a number of problematic connotations – the idea that essences must be intrinsic, unchangeable, immutable and have clear boundaries, for example. Most of these connotations are both undesirable and unnecessary for a discussion of kinds and in particular of *human* kinds. Fortunately, there is an independent way to appeal to an explanation of correlated features within different instances of a kind that does not need to draw on any talk of essences and hopefully has a much broader appeal.

The idea is simply that different instances share similar correlations of properties due to some single *common cause*. Wesley Salmon (1984) gives the example of two student essays. Imagine that you are handed two student essays. You discover that they are almost identical in their properties, to the extent that they even share some grammatical errors. Now consider two main hypotheses for this occurrence:

> (H.1) There are *two distinct causes* for the similarity between the two essays.
> (H.2) There is *a single common cause* for the similarity between the two essays.

Note that the second hypothesis does not give details about *the nature of* the common cause – say if one student copied the other, or if they both copied a common source off the Internet, for example. Yet, even without this specification, I think most of us would be inclined to say that the second hypothesis (H.2) is simpler and more plausible than the first (H.1).

There are a few different reasons for this. Not only does H.1 do little, if any, explaining of the similarity between essays (it rather makes it a matter of accident or chance), but H.2 also has more evidence stacked in its favor. Take, for instance, the same grammatical errors occurring in both essays:

this seems much more unlikely under H.1 than H.2. The probability that a *great number* of similarities would be shared – especially if they are not purposeful or functional – also seems unlikely if there was not a common cause (for a more detailed and critical discussion of common-cause explanations, see Sober, Chapter 2, 2015).

Now imagine a theory that postulates a common cause for the cluster of properties that different members of a *kind* share, say the individual horses belonging to the category *Horse*. Compare it with a theory that instead postulates *separate* causes for each individual horse's correlations of properties. Wouldn't we have similar reasons to favor the common-cause explanations also in this case? That is, wouldn't appealing to different causes for different horses' correlations of properties be less parsimonious than appealing to a shared cause between different horses?

We can thus state the **Common-Cause Principle for Kinds** as follows:

> It is more likely that rich correlations of properties occur in different instances, due to a common cause than due to separate causes.

Whether the common-cause principle indeed holds for kinds will depend on two features: first, it hinges on how strongly the proposed properties *correlate* in different instances, and second, it depends on whether the proposed common causes really do *explain* the correlations of properties. I have not said anything so far about whether these conditions in fact can be fulfilled in the case of human kinds,[12] but this is precisely what I will explore in the next two chapters. First, I will be investigating possible common-cause explanations in the existing literature on human kinds in Chapter 3, and then I argue for a historical-reproductive model of common causes in Chapter 4 and onward.

However, I suspect that some are not even prepared to go along as far as entertaining common causes for human kinds. The backlash against essentialism has been quite definitive here – in many cases, I might add, with good reason. In fact, it is becoming increasingly popular in philosophy of science to think of kinds without making many, if any, commitments about their explanation and sometimes denying an explanation of kindhood altogether. These positions can be associated with the original anti-essentialist arguments of John Locke: either there are *no* explanations of the correlations of properties shared among instances (the Sceptic, say) or there is no way of *knowing* whether there are common-cause explanations (the Agnostic, say).[13] The result is that any multiple projectability tends to be viewed as merely an outcome of an unexplainable "stable property cluster" (Dennett, 1991; Slater, 2015), a "brute fact" (Lewens, 2012) or a matter of "bare projectability" (Häggqvist, 2005; Häggqvist & Wikforss, 2018).

Such accounts seem to run into trouble in cases such as the category of *White horse*. It seems as if these accounts would give a problematic go-ahead to treating white horses as a kind. After all, individuals that fall under the category of *White horse* also share stable correlations (that is, the cluster of properties belonging to horses plus the property of whiteness). So, one might ask of those who think of the correlations as brute fact if categories like white horses are not just as real and just as good as putative scientific kinds. Instead, I contend that we could use the common-cause principle here: it seems more likely that there is a common cause of the property correlations belonging to the category *Horses* than there is in the category *White horses*, where the correlation with whiteness is purely definitional.

I therefore believe that these explanatory non-committal accounts lack the resources to distinguish epistemically unimportant categories from those categories that refer to kinds (for a more extensive critique against purely epistemic definitions of kinds, see also Lemiere, 2018). This is true not only for these accounts. In Chapter 3 (Section 3.3.1), I will argue that the popular purely causal kind account runs into similar problems.

Perhaps, then, one should *not* dismiss the application of the principle of common-cause explanation offhand (though more antiquated ideas of essences can indeed fall by the wayside).[14] To be sure, it would be wrong to suppose that there *always* are common causes of the property correlations; on occasion some shared properties may well be a matter of luck and separate causes. But the Sceptic and Agnostic make stronger claims than that. They make claims about *all* cases of property correlations among instances in the human sciences. This strikes me as unnecessarily dogmatic. Why not use both philosophy and relevant empirical sciences to investigate the possibility of common causes of candidate human kinds? That is what I propose to do in the chapters to follow, but let's first add some important moral and emancipatory motivations for such investigations.

## 2.4 Human kinds as levers for social change

The psychological sciences tend to approach human categories from quite a different perspective from the one described so far. Much of psychology is these days focused around the *harmful effects* of human categorization. This is perhaps unsurprising given the developments over the past century. Henri Tajfel – by many deemed the founding father of social psychology – recounts how his "fairly snug and secure" academic life was transformed by being a survivor of the Nazi German concentration camps (1981, p. 1). From Tajfel and colleagues in the field of social psychology, we have learned that even small and seemingly inconsequential cues of belonging to a category can trigger ingroup-outgroup thinking, like being allocated to an arbitrary category, say of a certain color. Recently both philosophers and psychologists have also focused a lot on implicit biases we have toward certain groups – biases that bypass our conscious awareness. They are deemed more important than explicit bias and more troubling as they seem to resist reflection and, many presume, change (however, see Travers, Fairhurst, & Deroy, 2020).[15]

Even more pertinent to this discussion, there is a worry about how deeper, more ontological committed views about human categories can trigger prejudice and wrongful discrimination. Social and cognitive psychologists have investigated what, on the level of the individual, prompts the development of essentialist ideas and how it can contribute to discrimination, implicit bias and harmful stereotyping.

This empirical work is clearly important, but it is not obvious what relationship there is between essentialist *thinking* – often termed *psychological essentialism* (Gelman, 2004) – and prejudice, xenophobia and the like. To be sure, there is some indication that essentialist thinking is not entirely innocuous. For instance, assigning salience to essentialist information seems to increase levels of prejudice and in-group bias, particularly among those holding recurring essentialist beliefs (Keller, 2005). And national identification and prejudice about nationalities other than one's own seems to depend on the degree to which subjects endorse an essentialist definition of their own nationality (Pehrson, Brown, & Zagefka, 2009).

Although such studies certainly demonstrate some of the harmful effects of psychological essentialism when it comes to human categories, I do not think it warrants a rejection of the possibility of human kinds or, for that matter, the idea that there are common causes. There are two reasons for this: the first has to do with the way essentialism tends to be operationalized in psychological studies such as the ones I just mentioned. In particular, the operationalization of essentialism often reflects a scientifically outdated view about the basis of human categorization. Essentialism here goes far beyond the assumption that kinds have common causes, specifying either that all members of a certain human category must share the same *biological ties*, in the form of genes or blood, or that they must share a more abstract intrinsic property that could be characterized as "deep", "immutable" and "unchanging". As shown in the following chapters, not only my own, but any serious contending account of human kinds flatly denies that members of human kinds can be united on this basis.

It would be interesting to see if a view on human categorization that is more convincing, both scientifically and philosophically, can avoid the pitfalls of traditional psychological essentialism (or at least the problems associated with existing operationalizations).[16] Hong and colleagues (2004) explicitly checked for such differences related to human categorization. They found that adopting a view that allowed members of an out-group to change their belonging alongside a more *inclusive* view of one's own in-group resulted in much less prejudice compared to the view of groups as unchanging and one's own group as exclusive. Recent work suggests that it might be perceived disloyalty among members of a group that underpins biased attitudes toward that group rather than any assumption about the basis for the category (Kunst, Thomsen, & Dovidio, 2019). That said, more work should clearly be done to identify the harmful components associated with essentialism and to establish whether a reformed view about the basis of human categorization can overcome the morally detrimental effects of out-group thinking, for example. So far, however, there is little evidence that the identification of common causes alone should be responsible for such effects.

The second reason for not allowing such work to lead to the wholesale rejection of common causes of human kinds is simply that social or cognitive psychology should not be allowed to settle such an account in the first place. To be sure, there are plenty of serious psychological and practical consequences of scientific and everyday practices of categorization. This does not imply, however, that the account or nature of human kinds should be fully determined by what we do with our categories. Finding answers concerning the basis of knowledge in the human sciences requires inquiry into the nature of the putative human categories *themselves*, not into the (mistaken) psychology that is attached to it.

All the same, I worry about an inquiry into human kinds that is purely justified by our quest for knowledge. This is because any putative knowledge in the human sciences is highly sensitive to what scientific projects a society and culture deem *valuable* in the first place. Perhaps some parts of the eugenics movement were motivated by naïve scientific curiosity about races, but the movement was surely also bankrupted by the political pressure to establish racial hierarchies and avoid any blending between races (e.g. Buchanan, Brock, Daniels, & Wikler, 2001). Thus, the desire for knowledge rarely drives investigations into human kinds *on its own*, but is typically supplemented by certain moral, aesthetic and political ideas (usually lumped together in philosophical jargon as "non-epistemic values").

If so, there might very well be a case for closing down any inquiry related to human kinds if there is a suspicion that the moral and political values driving such investigations are of a dubious character. Fortunately, I believe they are not. On the contrary, several important emancipatory aims are driving the quest for knowledge about human kinds and their putative common causes.

To start with, detecting patterns of comparative tendency within groups and differences between groups may well be the most important step in detecting patterns of *injustice*. Any case of injustices between certain groups or populations relies on first identifying real patterns of properties that vary between certain groups or populations (yes, they are rarely called kinds here, but the moral still holds). I mentioned earlier how generalizations such as "Young women are more likely than young men to go bust" tend to be combined with attempts at intervention. In fact, I believe these days much of the knowledge in the human sciences is actively fed into policies that purport to compensate for existing injustices. Of course, knowing that certain comparisons and generalizations hold will not be sufficient for policy: we will often need further facts about particular contexts and value-laden claims about why a pattern of difference counts as *unjust* before a particular policy can be endorsed.[17] My point here is only that if group or kind-based generalization had not been made in the first place, then there would arguably have been no need to think about why something is unjust to begin with.

This strategy also echoes the approach to human kinds adopted by Sally Haslanger in her recent book *Resisting Reality*:

> [I] argue throughout for the reality of social structures and the political importance of recognizing this reality. On the other hand, given that much of the (very real) social world consists of unjust social structures, I think this reality must be resisted. Another theme in the book is that one of the main goals of social constructionism is to lay bare the mechanisms by which social structures are formed and sustained so that we are better positioned to locate *the levers for social change*. We should not resist seeing the reality that we should, in fact, resist; in fact, disclosing that reality is a crucial precondition for successful resistance.
>
> (2012, pp. 30–31, emphasis added)

While I do not identify my own project as social constructivist, I fully agree with Haslanger's broader point: if reality is to be changed, then it first has to be disclosed. More precisely, in my view, locating the *levers of social change* starts with the uncovering of real (comparative) similarity and difference between groups. By extension, approaching reality as if we are all just members of the same human kind will not work if there are existing differences between individuals based on their membership of *different* kinds. This is a difference we may want to eliminate, or it may be something we deem irrelevant to justice (or something we want preserve). But to address it in one way or another, it is important we treat it as a real (comparative) difference that affects people's lives.

But what do the projects of locating the social levers of change have to do with providing common causes of human kinds? In response, I should first take care to distinguish between two different explanatory tasks (and two different levers of change): first, explanations of *specific* properties or generalizations and second, *common-cause* explanations of why the properties correlate or generalizations come together in different instances of a kind. The former type of explanation is probably one for the sciences. To be sure, explaining specific generalizations is far from trivial and may well involve conflicting theoretical and political perspectives. Take the generalization that women's businesses are more likely to go bust. Some scientists will propose certain structural features in the education and business climate that disadvantages women whereas others will propose that this might be partially due to innate sexual differences.

Where arriving at the right explanations of these specific generalizations is obviously important, it is neither necessary nor sufficient when we attempt to arrive at *common causes*. What one wants to know then is whether there is a common cause for why various, say, gendered properties (including a relative tendency to go bust) tend to come together in a particular gender *kind*. This is not the same task as explaining the emergence of single traits of a gender. Consider Salmon's student essay example again: the proximate explanation for a single property shared between the two essays – a common spelling mistake or the use of a particular reference – may indicate a common cause of the essays. But those single shared properties may still be accidentally shared among the two essays (i.e. there may be different causes for them in the two essays). What is more plausibly no accident is that multiple properties *come together* in both of the two essays.

Arriving at the right common-cause explanations of human kinds is also important for many very practical and emancipatory projects. It is also one in which I believe philosophers can play a role alongside scientists due to their capacity to synthesize empirical, theoretical and moral considerations. Armed with the correct common-cause explanation, one is in a better position to revise any mistaken (e.g. neurological or genetic) hypotheses of common causes. This would then also be an effective means for countering some existing biases in psychological essentialism. It is way easier to debunk pseudo-explanations of human kinds if one has an alternative account available (Guala, 2016, p. 139). Similarly, by not shying away from questions of common causes, one is also in a better position to toss out at least some of the baggage attached to psychological essentialism of human kinds.

But understanding the explanation for why properties of particular kinds come together – if indeed they do – is not merely of service as an epistemic corrective, important though that may be. As I will show in Chapter 7, this explanatory endeavor also has the potential of enhancing our understanding of how certain human kinds come to be associated with both historical and existing injustices and revealing why members of a kind may achieve a certain moral standing. The search for common causes of human kinds can therefore deepen our inquiry into human kinds and their role in both policy and political theory (see also Bach, 2016).

## 2.5 Summary

My point in this chapter has been to show that the central question about how empirical knowledge is at all possible in the human sciences depends on the existence of human kinds. We cannot hope for laws and universality in the human sciences, but we can hope for kinds that support rich correlations of properties or multiple projectability. I have shown that the existence of kinds, in turn, depends on some common causes that explain *why* correlations of properties come together in different members.

I have gone on to sketch some additional moral reasons to inquire into both human kinds and their putative common-cause explanations. To be clear, I have not denied that curiosity cannot in and of itself serve to justify the human sciences and projects concerning human kinds. I believe that knowledge has inherent value and that there should also be a degree of value freedom for scientists working in the human sciences, just as in all scientific inquiry. But because the quest for knowledge in the human sciences often arises from certain moral and political interests and is also put to use in policy, one should also offer explicit justifications for scientific inquiries that are of a moral character. Fortunately, I have argued that the scientific dealings with human kinds – both with the generalizations they support and with their putative common causes – are not uniformly negative from this perspective. Quite the contrary. Many of the scientific and philosophical projects regarding human kinds have the potential to be of an emancipatory nature in character.

## Notes

1 I follow Ruth Millikan (1998, 2000, 2017) in thinking that the basic purpose of these concepts (substance or unicepts) is *reidentification*; that is, recognizing that something is the same thing or belongs to the same kind as something else. But a defense of a particular understanding and function of kind *concepts* is beyond a monograph on human kinds. What I say should, for the most part, be compatible for other psychological theories of concepts and categories.

2 See Nancy Cartwright (2009) for a powerful and influential critique of this view of the nature of physics, however.

3 These statements are taken from *Hufvudstadsbladet* (a national Finnish daily newspaper), *The Economist* and the *Social Science Journal* (Johnson, Matthews, & Napper, 2016). Despite their factual basis, they should, of course, be taken as illustrations rather than central paradigms of (approximate) truths in the human sciences.

4 In my view, the fact that the sex/gender dimension is such a standardized way of checking difference between populations in all possible settings should give rise to a legitimate criticism about whether it is indeed a relevant dimension in

all the areas in which it is applied. I am grateful to Martin Bellander for making this salient to me.

5 Statements like this are also what Alexandrova (2018) has called "mixed claims" in that at least one of the values in the claim is dependent on moral or political values for their measurement (in this case, "victimization"). Like her, I don't take this inherent value-ladenness to undermine objectivity in the human sciences.

6 Leslie takes her examples of sharks and mosquitoes to show that some generics might be true in terms of conveying morally salient information (2008).

7 This ontological view that equates kinds with properties leads us to a very different story about human kinds but one which would take me too far afield to discuss in this book. See, however, discussions of kinds as multiply realized and as social institutions (Sections 3.1 and 3.2) for a sense of how this view might go.

8 For this reason, the kind horse fits our general-purpose learning mechanisms, and I would argue transcends particular classificatory projects in which classes are fitted according to a specific need or purpose (Millikan, 2017; cf. Dupré, 1995; Ludwig, 2018).

9 In fact, the domesticated horse is not regarded as a species itself but as a sub-species of *Equus ferus* (comprising both domesticated horses and the only extant wild horse, the Przewalski horse).

10 It is notable that one of John Stuart Mill's main motives for spelling out the methods and fallacies of inductive logic, including the importance of kinds, was for these principles to be applied in the life sciences – in the study of human nature – and in the moral sciences ([1886]1974, VI, 1, p. 833ff.). However, Mill denied that many *prima facie* human kinds, such as race and religious groups, were real kinds (Mill, System, I. vii. 4. Cf. IV. vi. 4., VI. xxii).

11 My colleague, Antonella Mallozzi, has usefully called answers to these questions *super-explanations* (2018), and we have – together with David Papineau – argued that these types of explanations have the force to underpin various modal claims (Godman et al., 2020). We show there is also a natural connection between super-explanations and the doctrine of essentialism.

12 One might already think there is a fundamental difference with the student essay example, since the similarities between instances of a human category can be quite weak. Indeed, they are often much weaker than in the discussed student essay cases. However, as I have argued in the beginning of this chapter, the notion of comparative tendencies is often sufficient in the human sciences, and the *multiple* projectability compensates for reliability of the generalizations in the case of kinds. Hence, I think the analogy has some *prima facie* interest.

13 There is some controversy in the scholarship on Locke about whether he denies real essences or just the possibility of acquiring knowledge about real essences. In any case, he believed that the explanations for the categories lay in their nominal definitions. For instructive discussions on Locke's view of kinds, see Ayers (1981), Hacking (1991) and Boyd (1991).

14 A prominent exception is in the philosophy of language: Saul Kripke (1980) and Hilary Putnam's (1975) causal theory of reference that assigns essences the extremely important task of fixing the references of natural-kind terms. Unfortunately, the scope of this book does not allow me to discuss the semantics and modalities of kind terms, although I am broadly sympathetic to the Kripke-Putnam account (see Godman et al., 2020).

15  The size of the effects of implicit biases are contested, but they have been demonstrated in a range of different areas, from consumer habits to political values to self-esteem (for a helpful history and review of the field, see Brownstein (2019); for a critical discussion see Gendler, 2011)).

16  See e.g. Haslam, Rothschild, and Ernst (2002), who distinguish among various aspects of essentialism and their differential force for prejudice.

17  Incidentally this is something I think many people can appreciate from their everyday life. As a child, when I observed that certain individuals, including myself and my Colombian and Finnish classmates, were barred from some games by our peers, I recognized that there was indeed *some* difference among us (different languages and social conduct) compared to the majority of our peers, but I also sensed that this difference should not have mattered for playing games with other kids.

# 3 Existing approaches to human kinds

The human sciences rely on categorization of humans, their traits and products into kinds. I defended this thesis in the last chapter with epistemic as well as with moral-political arguments. I also argued that an important condition for the existence of kinds is that their members are united by some common causes that explain why the properties of each member come together. So, what are candidate common causes in the case of human kinds?

This chapter explores some of the most influential accounts of human kinds in the literature. I should say right off the bat that these accounts have been developed with quite different concerns in mind than mine. Many, if not most, of the existing accounts of human kinds have been presented with the aim of assigning some autonomy to the human sciences vis-á-vis the natural and physical sciences. Reductionists such as Carl Hempel, Paul Oppenheim and Ernst Nagel have been very influential in pressing questions such as: how can one be sure that the subject matter, human beings and their kinds *really* are that different from kinds of other domains? Could it not be that the theories and kinds of the human sciences are ultimately reduced to a more fundamental level or scale?

Once the game has been set up this way, it seems you either must embrace physicalism and reduction or else spend your time attacking the reductive move head-on by suggesting some *marks of distinctness* for the human sciences and/or for human kinds. The first account I will review in this section claims that human kinds, like other special scientific kinds, are multiply realized. This makes them compatible with some forms of reduction, but also suggests some marks of distinctness. I then consider some accounts that focus on marks of distinctness that are not compatible with reduction: first, the tradition of social ontology, which suggests that human kinds are somehow explained via the existence of certain social institutions; and second, some popular naturalistic accounts of human kinds that each suggest subtly different marks of distinctness at the level of the mechanisms that realize the kinds.

The fact that the debate has been set up with a different concern in mind means that some – but not all – of the things these authors have to say about human kinds will be compatible with my own account, which I spell out in the following chapters. The purpose of this chapter is therefore really just as constructive as it is critical; I will assess some different accounts of human kinds and review whether there are any compelling lessons to draw from them.

The search for candidate common causes is still the main reason why I chose to discuss these particular accounts of human kinds over other possible candidates. Some accounts of kinds are, for example, not discussed because they reject common-cause questions outright: these include the epistemology-first and pluralist accounts that favor classification according to different scientific interests and domains of inquiry (see e.g. Dupré, 1995; Magnus, 2012). In fact, my argument in the last chapter about the epistemically and politically useful role for human kinds can be seen as my response to such accounts. Other accounts, e.g. classic essentialist accounts, are not discussed because they reflect a form of common-cause explanation for human kinds that seems too implausible in light of the current human and biological sciences. In addition, there are plenty of accounts focusing on *particular* human kinds such as gender, race and class. Some of these latter accounts will be discussed indirectly in this chapter (because what they say about a kind $K_1$ overlaps with what others say about kinds in general); others are discussed in the course of the case studies in the following chapters.

## 3.1 The multiple-realization account of human kinds[1]

The most straightforward counterargument to reductionism is Jerry Fodor's claim that some kinds are not reducible to physical kinds due to their *multiple realization* (1974). Though Fodor and others advocating multiple realization tend to concentrate on kinds in psychology as a paradigm, multiple realization is supposed to be the distinctive mark of kinds in all non-fundamental sciences such as chemistry, biology, or in Fodor's vocabulary, "special sciences" (henceforth abbreviated as SS (see e.g. 1974, p. 97).

The appeal of the multiple-realization thesis lies precisely in its potential to square physicalism or monism (i.e. the thesis that there is only physical stuff in the universe and not the stuff of souls and spirits, for example) with some justification for there being non-fundamental *sciences*. In essence, the multiple-realization thesis is simple. It is physicalist in terms of requiring that *some* physical state or kind $P_1$ must realize an instance of special science kind $SS_1$ (such that any system containing $P_1$ will necessarily also contain $SS_1$). It also holds that $SS_1$ is not *type-reducible* to an underlying physical kind. In other words, a disjunction of different physical kinds ($P_1$ _ $P_2$ _ $P_3$ _ . . . _ $P_n$) can realize $SS_1$. The type of examples that are typically discussed are generally psychological traits or categories like *Pain* and *Eye*, but the thesis of multiple realization is intended to have much broader application to all or most putative SS kinds.

But if SS kinds are not physical kinds, what, then, are kinds according to the multiple-realization tradition? Fodor speaks of kind terms as "bound variables in a proper special science laws" (1974, p. 102). But though he uses the language of laws, he claims SS laws are best understood as holding only *ceteris paribus* – that is, with exception (1974, ff.). So far, so good; nothing in the account seems to jar with what I have argued about human kinds earlier.

All the same, we should only want to tolerate an ample amount of exceptions to generalizations for some good reason. There must at least also be some (comparative) tendency and some stability across instances of a kind to begin with.

Yet now, those advocating multiple realization are drawn into the same questions of reduction all over again: why think that the different physical bases of an SS kind could end up producing stability across instances? This raises a dilemma for the non-reductive physicalist concerning the grounds for the apparent projectability of multiply realized kinds. This dilemma is described in slightly varying ways by Jaegwon Kim (1992), Ned Block (1997) and David Papineau (2009, 2010), but the common core is as follows:

### The Projectability Dilemma

1  SS kinds are both (a) projectable and (b) multiply realized.
2  Kinds are projectable only if each is realized by a single physical kind.
3  Kinds are multiply realized only if each kind is realized by multiple diverse physical kinds, i.e. $P_1, P_2, P_3, \ldots P_n$.

Claims 1–3 thus form an inconsistent set of propositions. The non-reductive physicalist wishing to maintain (1) cannot also hold on to both (2) and (3); hence the dilemma – one of the two has to be abandoned. Abandoning (3) is clearly not an option for the non-reductive physicalist. She must attempt to tackle (2). But (2) can only be rejected if the projectability of an SS kind can be explained in some way that does *not* depend on its being realized by a uniform physical kind or mechanism.

To be clear, Fodor's claim that the projectability need only be *ceteris paribus* is not of much help in dealing with this dilemma. If *ceteris paribus* laws are genuine empirical generalizations, then there must still be some reason for trusting them to begin with (Millikan, 1999; Papineau, 2009). Moreover, reductionist critics can always counter that the confidence placed in SS *ceteris paribus* laws is either unfounded or is ultimately explained by underlying physical laws.

So how can those that believe in multiple realization explain projectability? Is there something like a non-reducible common cause at work?

Whereas Fodor's original account is arguably one in which multiple realization is distinctive of the special sciences, more recently a less ambitious and more sensible version of the thesis seems to be at play: namely, that multiple realization is at least empirically possible and plausible for *some* kinds in the special sciences (Polger and Shapiro 2016).[2]

Both Ned Block and David Papineau have supported this latter, weaker thesis of multiple realization as an important empirical possibility in response to the aforementioned dilemma. They suggest that there are at least some interesting cases of multiple realization when a variety of different physical bases are selected to perform the same *function*. In the classic case of the category *Pain*, they suggest that the common selection processes explain the relevant stabilities and projectability across instances.

Consider my selection of vehicles to take me from London to Paris: I could travel by car and ferry; I could fly; I could take the train; and I could even combine any of these different modes of transport on various stretches of the journey. Hence, multiple vehicles can achieve the same result of getting from London to Paris. According to Block and Papineau, the appeal to different selection processes for the same function (travel from London to Paris in the example) provides a solution to the dilemma. What is offered is a defense not merely of multiple realization, but also of the projectability of human kinds via the selected function.

Why think that selection processes would yield multiple physical solutions to the same problem? Block (1997) suggests that *natural* selection is largely indifferent to the way in which beneficial results are achieved: if a particular effect or function is important enough for the fitness of the individual, then natural selection will even ensure that there are several different physical realizers for achieving the effect. In a similar vein, Papineau (2009, 2010) argues that *cultural* selection may well guarantee that there are different ways of achieving certain cultural and social ends that are particularly important for groups and individuals.

So, there seems to be good reason to expect that neither nature nor culture will be particularly discriminating when it comes to selecting the physical means required to perform a certain function, F. The important thing is that all of the different instances of a kind should have been selected to perform F. This is what guarantees their entering into specific *selection-based* lawlike generalizations. Thus, it would seem that it is possible to have it both ways: on the one hand, selection processes can bring about SS kinds that are genuinely multiply realized; on the other hand, the very same multiply realized kinds are projectable in virtue of supporting a particular generalization concerning their shared selected function.

Consider the category *Pain* – allegedly multiply realized and referring to an octopus state $M_1$, a human neural state $N_1$, a human neural state $N_2$ and so on. Papineau suggests that one can understand the category as denoting a naturally selected cross-species pain mechanism:

> It is widely supposed that pain is multiply physically realized across different life forms, yet nevertheless enters into laws mediating causes and effects, such as the law that bodily damage gives rise to pain and the law that pain in turn leads to avoidance of the source of the damage.
>
> (2010, p. 186)

Therefore, accepting Papineau's thesis that *Pain* is understood to refer to a cross-species pain mechanism – Pain$_1$ – that enters into two selection-based and closely associated laws produces a case of multiple realization. Crucially, any such selection-based category is projectable in a way that does *not* depend on uniform physical realization. The stability among instances of Pain$_1$ is simply indicative of the common selective pressures operating in different contexts, rather than of the same physical mechanism. In the terms of the preceding chapter, the selected function is the common cause.

I think there is good reason to restrain one's enthusiasm regarding the account of multiple realization that appeals to selected function. The reason is that the projectability of these selection-based categories is strictly limited to inferences concerning the selected function (and perhaps any design constraints imposed by that function). After all, on Papineau's account, for something to count as an instance of Pain$_1$, it merely has to function as a means to avoid bodily damage. While this leaves plenty of room for physical variability – a variety of states of different species and possible intelligent machines are likely to qualify as Pain$_1$ – the very permissiveness in terms of how an item is allowed to perform a function suggests that there will not be many commonalities among instances other than those that directly pertain to its selected function (such as how pain "feels" and the conditions by which pain can emerge). In other words, there are no grounds for assuming that instances of Pain$_1$ support any generalizations above and beyond those that are necessary for them to fulfill their functional role.

The upshot is that any categories defined purely in terms of their selected function support only single generalizations, or a very impoverished set. Mark Couch makes a similar point about the convergent evolution of the structure of the eye, emerging in different species as a way to respond to light:

> [I]t is hardly informative to be told that the eyes all function to respond to light. Researchers in vision science are concerned to discover more interesting empirical generalizations than this. Their interest is with finding generalizations that can be used to explain a broad range of

facts about the structures. The difficulty is that there is little more in common among the structures to be the basis of such generalizations. Given the differences that are present, there are only a limited number of generalizations about the eyes that hold across all the structures.

(2005, p. 1048)

Couch's point is that once items have been classified purely according to their selected function, there will be little else of interest for scientists to discover or uncover in terms of further similarities among instances. I urge that a similar moral holds for other categories defined purely on the basis of their selected function: the generalizations supported by these categories will be very few and unsurprising.[3]

This highlights the importance of a solution to the dilemma facing advocates of the multiple-realization thesis targeting categories that also support *multiple* empirical generalizations. The selected function as a common cause only guarantees one type of generalization; namely, the very function an item has been selected for. The criterion requiring SS kinds to support *empirical* generalization also rules out another recent attempt to defend multiple realization in the special sciences. Daniel Weiskopf suggests that an SS category might in some sense refer to a "functional kind" that supports functional generalizations in virtue of playing a role in *a range of well-confirmed models*. However, as he points out, whatever capacities and behavior are present must be "necessary effects" for the model(s) to hold true (2011, p. 246). Hence, although such models may in some sense ground functional categories in a way that allows them to enter into multiple lawlike statements, such statements will then have to be tied to the model *deductively*. Whatever the virtues of such "kinds", they do not support our ability to anticipate properties among new instances.

In sum, a selection-based solution to the dilemma fails to account for the possibility of multiply realized SS kinds. What is more, selection alone is a poor common cause for kinds in both biology and the human sciences, as it only supports one or a couple of generalizations. Indeed, if a central characteristic of kinds is that they instead support multiple empirical generalizations, as I have argued in the last section, it in fact follows that instances that are jointly projectable solely in relation to their selected function will not be genuine kinds at all (cf. Godman, Mallozzi and Papineau 2020).

A question lingers, however. Divorced from the claim about selected function, is multiple realization still a legitimate position for some human kinds? For all that I have argued, multiply realized kinds are still possible just not explained by common function. I will return to the issues of a multiple realization in relation to my proposal concerning historical kinds in

Chapter 6 (Section 6.2). For now, I hope to have convinced you that selected functions are not common causes of genuine kinds.

## 3.2 Human kinds as social institutions

Social ontology is another philosophical scene that has sprung from concerns to defend the irreducibility of the social sciences. The primary focus has been with social *institutions* such as hockey teams, senates and corporation boards, or particular instances of these institutions such as Helsingin IFK, the American Senate and the board of Airbnb. At first glance, institutions could be loosely regarded as kinds with people as their members and groups of institutions with individual institutions as their members. However, social ontologists are not foremost concerned with the shared tendencies of members of institutions or groups of institutions; they focus on explaining institutional *functions and structure* (Hindriks & Guala, 2015). Accordingly, one might think that two entirely different frameworks ought to be used to explain the different types of human groups – human kinds *proper* and institutions – and also the facts related to each group (see e.g. Ritchie, 2015). I believe this hunch reflects an existing division in the field at the moment (roughly between work on human and social kinds on the one hand and social ontology and social institutions on the other).

I am not convinced that one should go for such a division of labor right off the bat, however. Given that the topics tend to be discussed in different philosophical corners, I believe there is a risk that the demarcation between these fields is assumed rather than based on any substance. Where should the line between *institutional functions or facts* and *empirical generalizations* be drawn in the first place, for example, and are there genuinely different explananda at stake? As I shall show in this section, this has not been clearly argued for and is needed if we should evoke relevant differences between empirical facts and institutional facts.

My task in this section is therefore to investigate a particularly influential account of social facts by John Searle and a more recent yet related formulation proposed by Francesco Guala. These authors serve as appropriate discussion targets because they expressly wish to develop a *unifying framework* to explain *all* social facts either as institutional facts or as "fallouts" from institutional facts (Searle, 2010, p. 117) or stemming from certain equilibria of strategic games (Hindriks & Guala, 2015; Guala, 2016).[4] I purport to show that these frameworks of social ontology may not achieve the unification in the philosophy of the social sciences to which they aspire. All the same, these accounts also reveal how human kinds either initially can possess or are capable of acquiring relevant normative properties such as status functions – a point I will return to in Chapter 7.[5]

### 3.2.1 *Human kinds as a product of collective recognition*

Like Fodor, John Searle also starts from the challenge of how social facts can emerge in a world governed by physical laws. His focus is on the social world, and in his view language and in particular speech acts have a privileged role in the creation of social facts.

Searle's springboard is speech-act theory, which he developed on the basis of J.L. Austin's work *How to Do Things with Words* (1962; Searle, 1969). The central and largely uncontroversial tenet of this body of work is that communication is more about *making things happen* than about representing things to one another. In relation to the emergence of social facts, Searle thinks we should focus on speech acts that combine features of representing the world as it is with utterances that match one's desires. In classic terms, these linguistic acts have two directions of fit (Anscombe, 1957): on the one hand getting the mental state to fit with the world as it stands (representing the world), and on the other hand getting the world to fit one's mental state (ensuring that the world, as a result, has the properties stated by the utterance).

How does this happen? According to Searle, this can happen when an official at a presidential inauguration declares, "Barack Obama is the president of the United States of America". She simultaneously represents this fact but also makes it the case. Such utterances are *declarations* (Searle, 2010, p. 11 ff.). Other examples are "quasi-speech acts" where declarations are encoded in rules, constitutions, tests and certifications. So, in Searle's view, social or institutional facts emerge via the ability of speech acts to perform this dual role of *representing* and *making things the case*. In short, thanks to language, things are possible that would otherwise not be possible in a physically constituted world.

But in order for speech acts to work, there also has to be some *uptake* that give speech acts their "illocutionary force" (Searle, 1969). Here Searle connects speech-act theory with the growing literature on collective intentionality (Epstein, 2018). The statement "Barack Obama is now president" would not be successful in its (dual) mission according to Searle if it did not also occur against a background of collective acceptance, or what he has later come to refer to as *collective recognition* (2010, 56 ff.), thereby emphasizing the fact that it may not be a matter of explicit endorsement. In his famous example about facts about money, it means that "each participant accepts the existence and validity of money in the belief that there is mutual acceptance on the part of others" (ibid., p. 58).

What, then, does a group or collective need to recognize *about* Obama and money for there to be institutional facts? Connected to Obama's presidential role, these are clusters of certain rights, obligations and duties and as related to money, the value inherent in coins and credit cards. These properties are what Searle calls the *status functions* (or *deontic powers*) of President Obama and different instances of money. Declarations wield their power in a physical universe by assigning a status function to a range of other items such as groups of individuals (e.g. hockey teams), objects (e.g. courts of justice) and landscapes (e.g. borders). These properties are *epistemologically objective*, but they are also *ontologically subjective* since their creation and maintenance are ultimately due to a collective's recognition.

But does the account really speak to the generalizations, projectability and empirical knowledge that I have argued are the bread and butter of the human sciences? Let us try out Searle's framework for understanding some social facts about young women, men and doctors (introduced in Section 2.1). What relevant declarative acts are recognized by a collective in such cases? That certain groups of individuals are declared to be, and recognized as, "young women", "young men" and "doctors" seems unproblematic, but what status functions follow from such declarations? For there to be status functions, there must also be certain *properties* ascribed to the relevant individuals or groups of individuals in speech acts. And then there must be collective uptake of these utterances. But for what properties of gender and occupation might it be possible to achieve general recognition?

The issue here is not the scarcity of declarations that aim to ascribe certain properties to individuals, such as certain gender roles – there are plenty. However, such declarations generally seem to represent points of collective dispute rather than recognition. Most purported social properties or functions of gender, say, are bound to be resisted by someone, and why should that someone be *a priori* excluded from a collective? Moreover, even if it is assumed that some suitably mild recognition is present for some status functions to be *established*, it will still be difficult to maintain over the course of time (recall that one of the aims is to explain not merely the emergence but also the maintenance of social institutions). Suppose it was once collectively accepted that women are innately prone to hysteria; surely that is regarded as a dubious stereotype by our collective mindset today (if there ever was one; cf. Fricker, 2007).

But perhaps the scope of Searle's framework should be limited: perhaps it only applies to groups that are more clearly reliant on some kind of institutional practice. Medical doctors, for instance, might seem to be a better case for Searle and others advocating the strategy of explaining social facts by means of collective acceptance or intentionality. After all, there seems to be a whole host of declarations and legitimizing practices for someone to count as a doctor – including certain national certifications, examinations and memberships of certain professional bodies. A plausible case could be made for such quasi-speech acts simultaneously performing the role of representing and changing the world such that doctors would acquire the status functions necessary for them to perform their professional role.

In fact, the reason why professionals such as medical doctors and lawyers at least initially seem to fit well into Searle's framework may actually be that they have some particularly desirable and commonly accepted roles to play in society to begin with (note that this is probably not the case for all or most human kinds, let alone all that fall under the category of a profession, such as philosophers). However, whether or not some groups possess *some* collectively recognized status functions, most relevant *facts* about professional groups are not good candidates. Recall that the example was that doctors, as a group, are more likely than any other professional group to commit suicide. Yet it would be absurd to claim that there is any collective intentionality let alone collective recognition of this fact! Indeed, the discoverable empirical facts do not seem to be particularly socially functional at all (in the sense that they serve some social or cultural purpose by which one can hope to achieve collective agreement). Instead, I have argued, the generalizations and comparisons that are common stock in the human sciences represent tendencies, but hardly *purposeful* tendencies among individuals of a kind.[6]

In fact, Searle admits that many social facts are not directly collectively recognized status functions. Some, he suggests, are "discovered fallouts" (2006, 84f.; 2010, 117f.). He gives the example of a discovered fact or comparative tendency about baseball batters, namely that "left-handed baseball batters are statistically better than right-handed batters", and acknowledges that "this is not part of the rules of baseball; nor the result of collective intentionality" (2006, p. 84). Still, Searle claims, facts like these are not autonomous of his scheme of institutional facts, but are rather outcomes that, although not envisioned by the (constitutive) rules, "happen[s] once the rules are in play" (ibid., p. 85). They are then somehow the results or consequences of prior institutional facts.

But how do constitutive rules such as the rules of baseball have any bearing on discoverable facts such as the relative superiority of left-handed batters? At first glance, the most straightforward explanation of this particular fact concerning batters seems to be down to the dynamics of human movement rather than any social facts. Perhaps, though, the relative superiority of left-handed baseball batters is down to the institutional biases that favor left-handedness in terms of practice and, say, batting design.[7] Still, this type of institutional arrangement does not seem to be what Searle had in mind in referring to them as systematic fallouts. What seems to matter to him is that a relevant collective must first accept or recognize that baseball batters can be ascribed certain status functions (such as being a base runner, and able to drive or advance other runners). But any status functions of baseball players seem irrelevant to explanations of the relative superiority of left-handed batters. To be sure, the emergence of institutional facts about baseball and batters may be a condition for the very existence of the game, but the question remains: how do discoverable facts simply "fall out" from this existence?[8]

### 3.2.2  Human kinds as a product of stable equilibria

As the connection between status functions and discoverable social facts remains oblique on Searle's account, one might want to turn to a recent alternative proposal concerning social institutions from the game theoretical tradition put forward by Francesco Guala. Here social institutions and the related facts are explained by certain *stable equilibria* of strategic games. According to Guala, it is not through speech acts and collective recognition that institutions and institutional change occurs, but rather it is through a certain *change of equilibrium*. According to the game theoretical tradition, a change in equilibrium and emergence of social facts does not need to evoke collective attitudes other than the *cumulative change of preferences and expectations* that shift an existing balance of behavior.

Might new equilibria, then, account for the emergence of discoverable facts – or, as Guala puts it, *behavioral regularities* – attached to human kinds? Guala seems to think so, and gives the following stylized account of how this would work when there is a change in the behavioral regularities of being gay:

> [S]uppose that a new term ("gay person") is introduced, to express a new conception of the same sexual orientation. Suppose that a number of people who preoccupy prominent roles in society (artists, designers and musicians) begin to self-identify as gay. If "gay" connotes a positive, legitimate, interesting way of life rather than a moral defect or medical condition, people's preferences and propagation functions may change significantly. . . . A minority of activists could for example cross the tipping point, persuading others to follow. . . . The new label changes beliefs about classified people, beliefs change behavior, and so forth, until a new identity is stabilized in the superior equilibrium.
>
> (2016, p. 141)

While there is nothing particularly wrong with modeling such cases as a change in equilibrium, the question is: what does the achievement of a stable equilibrium really *explain*? In fact, it seems that any *explanatory* work in Guala's account relies on the cumulative change in preferences within a relevant community. Hence Guala – just like Searle – also believes that our attitudes taken together, or in conjunction, explain emergent behavioral regularities and thus the emergence of new discoverable facts about human kinds. The account then does not seem to amount to much of a different explanatory framework than Searle's after all.

Both accounts also encounter problems with fixing the *identity* of a collective (or in the case of Guala's approach, of the group with a cumulative change of preferences).[9] In response to Amie Thomasson's criticism that a collective attitude is often redundant in explanations – she gives the example that a "society has the additional feature of being racist, without the need for anyone to accept any constitutive rules regarding racism" (Thomasson 2003, p. 287) – Searle offers a rare account of how he thinks one should fix the identity of a community responsible for the collective recognition. Although he agrees with Thomasson that a community can be described as racist without its members collectively accepting the term for themselves, he still believes that for a community to be racist there has to be *some* community that assigns "deontic facts to a (different) community based on race" (2010, p. 118). What Searle presumably means is that racism in a community is a fallout of the ability of a group in a society to (mistakenly) assign racialized properties to another group (Searle acknowledges that status functions may be based on false beliefs). The former group is racist (Rac) and the latter is racialized (rac), thus rendering discoverable facts about a racist society.

This proposal about Searle's basic status functions is awkward. Is the explanation for any deontic powers or status functions belonging to the racialized group (rac) really their being racialized by some *other* collective (Rac)? Racist societies such as apartheid regimes certainly tend to impose certain prescriptions for what racialized groups can do; how they can move, live, work and so on. What is strange, however, is that such status functions should be explained via the collective *recognition* of another group (e.g. Rac). It seems the real explanatory work in the example goes via the power structures present in the society, such that members of Rac are able to *decide* how members of rac should lead their lives. In fact, it is only when one knows something about these power differences between certain groups and their expressions that one is able to determine which the relevant collectives are and what the candidate status functions are. By that time any collective attitudes towards properties of groups seem rather redundant (hence, we are back to Thomasson's concern about why collective attitudes are required for describing discoverable facts).

Even the appearance of institutional facts recognized by a relatively silent and passive collective often masks implicit power dynamics by means of which one group asserts itself over another. In his critique of Searle, social scientist Ignacio Sánchez-Cuenca, for example, argues that before the East European revolutions, institutional facts largely reflected the power and imposition of a minority, or the absence of organization and agency within the majority (2007, 180f.).

What then are the lessons to be learned from Searle's and Guala's attempts to provide a general explanatory framework for explaining social facts? First, many social facts are not institutional facts. Searle's more recent attempt to accommodate discoverable social facts within his framework as *fallouts* from prior institutional facts does not help. At the very least there is an explanatory gap in terms of how to get from status functions to discoverable generalizations. Guala's attempt to provide explanations of discoverable facts in terms of changes in stable equilibria is not much of an improvement. In fact, many institutional facts about norms and functions are not simply a matter of (majority) collective recognition (or cumulative changes of preferences). Rather, these facts belie intricate power relations between groups. What is more, a proper analysis of their emergence may well reveal that any "collective recognition" is simply redundant in an explanation.

Despite these shortcomings, the institutional and game theoretic framework both draw our attention to a different class of social facts than the empirical generalizations that I have stressed so far. This has two main implications going forward. First, there clearly are institutional facts – about norms, permissions, obligations assigned to individuals, groups and entities in society. These facts, of course, will also be of interest in the social sciences in their own right. Second, some groups and categories, initially associated with certain status functions and deontic powers, might become kinds supporting empirical generalizations (e.g. medical doctors) and *vice versa*, some human kinds might acquire status functions (as I will argue in the case of ethnicity in Chapter 7).

All the same, it is problematic to use an explanatory framework of status functions that simply posits some collective of individual preferences (Guala) or of group recognition (Searle). These collectives need to be unpacked. When they are, one usually ends up homing in on the relevant groups and institutions of power. Many status functions simply rely on legislature, such as in the case of state-sanctioned apartheid or, more positively, of anti-discrimination legislation aimed at promoting opportunities for certain genders and minority groups. Others follow the norms and conventions imposed by a powerful group in a society, and yet others reflect a tacit majority agreement about manners. In this sense the focus on collective recognition and the cumulative changes in preferences misses the point. The real action lies in the power asymmetries concerning *whose* acceptance, *whose* preferences and *whose* speech matters to how status functions emerge. It seems to me that social scientists interested in explaining status functions are better off just starting with identifying the particular groups and power relations responsible for certain status functions and norms.

## 3.3 Human kinds in reaction to the natural kind tradition

The accounts reviewed so far have not had much to say about common causes – causes that explain not merely single generalizations, but *kinds* whose instances jointly support the same property correlations and *multiple projectability*. This explanatory concern has, however, been in sight for those who have built their accounts of human kinds either out of or in reaction to the natural kind tradition.

It is useful to begin with an exchange from 1991 between Ian Hacking and Richard Boyd. The authors asked what might be salvaged from the natural kind tradition in a modern and naturalistic – as in a continuous-with-science – framework. They were concerned with natural kinds in general, but the discussion also proved particularly influential for the way *human* kinds have been understood since. Although both authors agreed on the importance of *social processes* for explaining human kinds, Hacking sided with Fodor and Searle in rejecting the idea that human kinds could simply be modeled on natural kinds: "Most 'human kinds' – kinds of people and their behavior – are social *rather than* natural kinds" (1991, p. 123, emphasis added), whereas Boyd subscribed to the view that "there are extremely good reasons for treating many property-cluster kinds and social kinds, and the terms that refer to them, on the model of natural kinds and natural kinds terms" (1991, p. 129).[10]

I will start with the accounts of human kinds that have grown out of this exchange, beginning with Boyd's, followed by Hacking's account. Finally, I will consider Ron Mallon's recent constructivist account of human kinds, which draws on both Hacking's and Boyd's work.

### 3.3.1 Kinds as a product of causation and homeostasis

Richard Boyd has developed a compelling account of kinds designed to fit with realist concerns on the one hand, and to cover a broad variety of scientific fields – including even the moral sciences (!) – on the other (1991, 2010). In Boyd's view, what *defines* this family of kinds is the *cluster of properties* that co-occur for each kind and the *homeostatic mechanisms* that bring about the co-occurrence (1991, p. 141). This definition does not yield a distinction in kind between the natural sciences and the human sciences, which is also why he resists the idea that natural and human kinds differ in principle from one another.

Boyd's proposal also contains a common-cause element: what explains a kind is any *homeostatic (H) mechanism* that sustains a particular *property cluster (PC)* – hence, the account is often termed the *HPC account*, and I will at times use this abbreviation myself. The term "homeostasis" comes from cybernetics and refers to the tendency of a system to return to a normal state despite relative disturbances, yet Boyd's paradigm examples are from biology, such as a species' phenotypic properties being sustained over time by interbreeding and the exchange of genetic material (1991).

One salient idea is that a class of causal mechanisms are also homeostatic in character. They explain the cluster of "derivative" properties of a kind. At other times Boyd stresses that the *properties within the cluster* can also have a role in sustaining or constraining the homeostasis (1999). In that case, what at least partly explains the cluster is presumably the inertia in, or feedback between, the properties themselves. Followers of Boyd have since placed different emphasis on the mechanistic side of his proposal on the one hand (Kuorikoski & Pöyhönen, 2012) and the feedback of the properties themselves on the other (Slater, 2015). Recently, Muhammad Khalidi has explicitly argued for a combination of these positions. Kinds, in his view, are just highly connected nodes in causal networks, which sometimes are explained by causal mechanism and other times by feedback process and yet other times, both (2018). In what follows I will, like Khalidi, assume that the mechanistic and feedback accounts can be combined in some causal explanatory framework.

It is usually emphasized as a virtue of these accounts that the relevant generalizations, e.g. in the case of species, need not be perfect precisely because the relevant causes or mechanisms do not perfectly sustain the relevant properties in each instance of the kind. This also fits nicely with my view earlier that kinds can support multiple generalizations, but each generalization may be quite weak to the extent that it may be merely a matter of comparative tendency. The unreliability of the causal mechanisms involved might also seem like a decent explanation for this. But if weak generalizations are to be expected *given* certain causal mechanisms, then it would be good to know what these mechanisms are more precisely. For Boyd and his followers, *the type and nature* of the relevant causal, and possibly homeostatic, mechanisms responsible for the property clusters is usually thought to be independently established by science as well as by more specific fields of science (such as in psychology and biology). Fair enough, but in the present context in thinking about possible common causes of *human* kinds, one may wish for some more specificity about which *type of* properties or mechanisms count as common causes.

As I mentioned earlier, the case that Boyd discusses in most detail is that of species, where he originally suggested that the homeostatic mechanisms are interbreeding and the exchange of genetic material – at least in sexually reproducing species (1991). Boyd has since gone on to amend this also to include exogenous environmental factors such as the reference to selection pressures (1999, 2010). Indeed, these causal factors or mechanisms are likely to be involved in sustaining the typical traits of at least sexually reproductive species. But if you are to generalize from the case of species to human kinds, it seems that something more should be said about *why* some causes are homeostatic or count as causal explanations of certain property clusters.

Perhaps, in Khalidi's terms, some nodes are simply more highly causally connected whereas others are not, and at a certain cut-off point they form kinds. But there are also plenty of nodes in causal networks that are highly connected which one may *not* wish to include as kinds. In the case of white horses, for example, there might be causal mechanisms that sustain the similarity in horsiness among members and, in addition, the shared *pigmentation* (in this case, fur) that accounts for the specific wavelength-selective that reflects light. The category *White horse* then seems to be a very well-connected node. However, as explained in the previous chapter, white horses do not constitute a kind, or at least not a kind of scientific concern, because there is very little to learn about them that is not already covered by the superior category *Horse*.

It bears mentioning that Boyd and some of the authors behind these causal models of kinds have a soft spot for the pluralist idea that specific scientific *domains and disciplines* get to accommodate or determine what the relevant causal kinds are for their specific inquiry (Boyd, 1991; Magnus, 2012). This type of pluralism typically implies that as long as there is some measure of scientific success, different disciplines and classificatory practices get to determine which property clusters and which causes count.[11] It is certainly true that the category, *White horse* is not part of a successful science, but what we are really after is an explanation of this fact. Is it just a contingent matter that white horses are not of scientific interest? I believe it is not *just* up to the disciplines to decide which property clusters concern them. There is something in the world that imposes the right constraints. What could that be? As Mohan Matthen also notes in the case of white horses, Boyd's "HPC theory leaves the question open, and offers no guidance on how to decide" (2012, 139; see also Reydon, 2009).

What I do think these authors get right is that in searching for common-cause explanations of kinds, one should be looking for causes and mechanisms that have some *independent* support in the relevant area of scientific study (as in the case of species). The problem is just that it is *not sufficient* to say that discipline-relevant mechanisms need to contribute to homeostasis within a cluster or that they are highly connected causal nodes. Something more is needed to count as a common cause explanation.

### 3.3.2 The looping effects of human kinds

There are many reasons to devote attention to Ian Hacking's "looping" or "moving target" account of human kinds. It is perhaps the most well-known account of human kinds. It also suggests social and psychological mechanisms for human kinds that are left unspecified in Boyd's account. And it can be seen to offer a bridge from institutional facts, which we have seen are the focus of social ontology, to discoverable facts.

In a rich series of papers and books, Hacking demonstrates how institutional change in scientific, typically medical, concepts and diagnostics leads to changes in the human kinds *themselves*. In fact, it is not only a matter of change in the relevant kinds, but it can also be a matter of *creating* new kinds of people (2007a). At the core of all Hacking's illuminating case studies lies the idea that one's own beliefs and motivations about belonging to a category (as well as the beliefs of others) induce changes in behavior. If one believes that one falls under a category, such as *Autism*, and it is also something that has a certain moral valence (it is either something we want to be or *not* want to be), this will affect one's behavior. Eventually these actions amount to changes not only in individual behavior, but also in the population of people deemed to belong to the category and thus, eventually, to the kind itself. Finally, Hacking argues, this means a change in the relevant *science* of the kind. There is thus a feedback loop between category-person-category. These series of changes constitute the famous "looping effects" of human kinds (1995).

This means that Hacking's model goes beyond the "labeling effects" that sociologists typically identify within the labeling theory (Scheff, 1984). There are *many other* ways in which belonging to a category can affect behavior – not just by being labeled in a certain way. In the case of autism, for example, Hacking points to external factors such as the complex bureaucracies that pick out individuals with autism in the early years of schooling as well as the creation of organizations like the Autism Society of America that are responsible for triggering certain changes to what it means to be a person with autism (Hacking, 2007a). Nor does Hacking in his account of looping effects commit to a particular attitude that people must have towards a kind for it to undergo looping (Searle's speech act followed by collective *recognition* and Guala's cumulative change in preferences and expectations are certainly examples of change that can prompt looping).[12] What matters more for Hacking is that the category has some *moral worth* or valence – not a particular type of valence.

It is true that Hacking tends to discuss cases where people become motivated to *conform* to how they are expected to behave when they belong to a category. Nonetheless, a group of patients may also reject the way in which medical professionals classify them, for example. Hacking argues that when "homosexual" was used as a medical classification connected to legal punishment, it was a category that people resisted and actively rebelled against. As Guala noted earlier, only later did this lead to a movement aspiring to take control of the category and reinstill a sense of pride in the individuals who fell within it (Hacking, 2007a). In such cases we seem to witness the alteration of the classification, and the beliefs associated with it, in a reaction against the scientifically sanctioned use. The looping effect then manifests as a self-*defeating* loop rather than a self-*fulfilling* loop (Khalidi, 2009).

In fact, Hacking's many different case studies have demonstrated how different scientific and institutional triggers of a particular time and diagnosis can all affect psychological and social responses to a categorization. Another dimension that matters is what (moral) attitudes there are toward belonging to a particular kind. For Hacking, then, looping or feedback effects are always dependent on the particular *moral and ecological niche* in which the human kind and category exists. As such, the looping also takes quite different trajectories depending on factors such as the institutions present, the moral valence, and the novelty and attraction of a category.

This also means that Hacking's story of looping effects is very difficult to apply as a *sui generis* account of human kinds. As Jessica Laimann (2020) argues, for example, some looping mechanisms contribute to the stability of the properties originally associated with a kind, whereas others undermine it. Moreover, she suggests one is often mistaken about the *mechanisms* responsible for stabilizing or destabilizing the properties in question: one may, to use her example, think there is some biological mechanism responsible for the stabilities of a particular gender when, in reality, there are complicated social-cultural-feedback mechanisms at play. Finally, even establishing that there is *some* looping or feedback involved when a group of individuals reacts to being categorized does not provide much guidance as to how large these effects are and what properties of the kind they will affect. One consequence is that it is not clear if one should regard looping as a problem for stable scientific research, categorization and policy in the human sciences. Indeed, if science and policy want to track the effects of looping and determine the extent of the problem, then a much more fine-grained classification of looping mechanisms is needed.[13]

In fact, in many ways Hacking's prime interest is not in specifying social or psychological mechanisms for looping: instead, he tends to emphasize the various *institutional* and *cultural vectors* that play a part in determining the trajectory. In *Mad Travelers* (1998), for example, Hacking describes what could be the first diagnosed case of hysterical fugue or compulsive wandering. Albert Dadas, a native of the Bordeaux region in France, suffered from memory loss followed by a strange urge that led him to travel obsessively, without having much sense of where and why. According to Hacking, there are four principal vectors in the *moral-cultural niche* that affect the development of mad travelling into a short-lived epidemic: (1) the medical taxonomy at the time; (2) a cultural polarity between romantic tourism and criminality; (3) observability and salience (the condition was noticeable, strange and disturbing); and (4) the sense of relief and understanding the condition nevertheless granted.

Now, there is no doubt that the moral and cultural niche in which a condition develops affects the prevalence, stability and the expression of certain medical and psychiatric syndromes (see also Godman, 2016b). What I doubt is whether the explanations of prevalence and expression, be they cultural, psychological or social, count as *common causes* of why different members of a particular human kind share a cluster of properties.

Let us take the case of compulsive wandering. Although not always reaching epidemic proportions, the same condition can clearly emerge in quite distinct niches and conditions. By way of an anecdote, I encountered two potential cases (one admittedly fictional) one summer in the early 2000s. At the time I was reading Alan Warner's novel *The Man Who Walks*, which chronicles a nephew's attempt to track down his amnesiac criminal uncle who is "mad travelling" in the highlands of Scotland. The features of this uncle do not differ much from that of Hacking's Albert Dadas. At the time I was reading the book, I also met a visitor at the local agricultural history museum in which I was working who had wandered all over the Northern Hemisphere with no end or mission in sight. As I recall, he also did not remember what had instigated the travel or much of what his life had looked like prior to the journey. I brought him back to my family home to use our shower, and he was offered to stay a few nights in our playhouse. I have to say my mom was quite relieved when he suddenly took to his travels again after an extended stay at our farm.[14]

This supposed shared cluster of properties in these different cases of compulsive wandering calls out for an explanation despite obvious variations in expression and prevalence over time and place. On an abstract level, one certainly might characterize many mechanisms as having the same looping or feedback structure – as have others concerned with reactivity, performativity and self-fulfilling prophecies in the social and psychological sciences. The question of how these abstract mechanisms can be unpacked remains however. We might want to know at what level these feedback mechanisms predominantly operate, if they stabilize properties, and if they have a large effect or not. Although these are all promising lines of inquiry, they hardly constitute an investigation into common causes of human kinds. The mechanisms seem too multifarious and capricious for that role (Laimann, 2020). And it could even be that the common cause of a kind is also entirely different from those that account for any looping effect a kind has undergone or will undergo.

Nevertheless, on the population level (for the frequency of cases found within a particular population), as well as for the precise expression of a condition, Hacking is surely right in claiming that the cultural-moral niche matters a great deal. What is more, I am not ruling out the possibility that the cultural-moral niche can help us locate the common cause of the cluster of properties belonging to a kind. Indeed, some of Hacking's ideas about how a niche matters will live on in my own proposal. Before I get to that, however, I will review a more recent proposal put forward by Ron Mallon that incorporates Hacking's and Boyd's work while also suggesting some novel candidate common causes.

### 3.3.3  Naturalist social constructivism

Whereas Hacking's work on human kinds does not have much ambition of providing anything like *a* model of human kinds, Ron Mallon quite explicitly does: "My aim is to articulate an account of the construction of causally significant human-kind categories that is both general and possible" (2016, p. 68). Like Searle and Hacking (on occasion), Mallon describes himself as a social constructivist about human kinds. For Searle constructivism is expressed through the influence of language and collective recognition in constructing social facts about groups. For Hacking the cultural and moral niche constructs by shaping an awareness of belonging to a kind, which in turn shapes behavior, the kind and the rest of the loop. Mallon's constructivism, instead, builds primarily on the *psychological representation of certain categories* and how it causes the construction of human kinds. With this focus, in Mallon's work, we do find something close to a common-cause explanation located at the level of individual and collective representations.

In contrast to Hacking, Mallon emphasizes the representations of *others* rather than those who allegedly belong to a category – in other words, how out-groups shape the formation of human kinds. He argues that once different agents have certain representations of a category, a belief or a desire that a person of a category should behave in a certain way, it is then quite intentional and rational for agents of that category to modify their action in accordance with the representations of others. If I represent a certain gender or ethnicity, I will also have certain expectations in certain social situations, and Mallon claims it is rational for others to behave in line with such expectations. According to Mallon, conforming to representations may be either *strategic*, such as when you gain support and recognition from the community by behaving in a stereotypical fashion, or *non-strategic*, where there is no obvious social benefit.[15]

Mallon also provides examples of when the change caused by a representation is *self-directed*. Social psychologist Carol Dweck studied how one's beliefs about one's own capacities – as fixed or capable of growth, for example – influence one's performance. She suggests that beliefs about stereotypical behavior of a group, such as one's gender, influence performance: if prior to taking a maths test, one is made conscious of being a woman, and this is represented as a fixed or innate trait, for example, one performs worse than if one were not made aware of it (Dweck, Chiu, & Hong, 1995).

One advantage of Mallon's proposal to focus on psychological representations is that it narrows Hacking's explanatory claims to the particular ways in which the other- or self-directed representations can guide behavior: they basically *conform* with existing representations and common knowledge. On this basis, Mallon argues that constructed human categories can achieve stability over time (2016, p. 162 ff.), thereby turning his focus away from the cases Hacking describes in which people act in a contrary manner to what is expected of them.[16]

Like Hacking, however, he realizes that psychological explanations will only go so far. Thus, he agrees that the construction of human-kind categories also derives from the surrounding environment, or cultural niche, that Hacking describes. In Mallon's terms, environmental construction "scaffolds" the acquisition of some representations rather than others. One of the scaffolding mechanisms that he has in mind is the cultural network to which the individuals belong and through which they share knowledge. Another is the norms surrounding the use of space, as in the case of racial segregation in the US, where differential historical zoning and norms about house purchasing set people up to behave according to the categories of a certain spatial location.

There thus seem to be quite a few mechanisms, psychological and environmental, that determine the representations and thus explain the stable properties of human kinds in Mallon's account. A particular human kind such as a race may acquire many of its properties from different sources: some from conforming to the stereotypes of other's representations, some properties from the common knowledge of the networks of which perceived members are a part, and yet others from the material and spatial conditions of those represented as belonging to a particular racial category.

These are certainly plausible causal pathways that make certain generalizations about human kinds true, as Mallon also claims. The problem with introducing such a range of proximate mechanisms for different properties of a kind such as race is that it moves us further away from a common-cause explanation. A conjunction of different properties, each of which explains a different feature of race, is just that: a list of different properties explaining different racial properties. This leaves us once more with an unexplained set of correlations – why are all those different racial properties found to correlate with one another? To put things bluntly, a range of proximate mechanisms implies *no* explanation at all as to why the properties *come together* in each instance of a purported race.

Racial segregation may, for instance, be explained by historical zoning and norms. The tendency to conform with positive stereotypes might be best explained by the common knowledge of one's network, whereas conforming with negative representations might be due to automatic responses to discriminatory attitudes.[17] Yet these explanations do not jointly explain why these features *cluster* together in the instances of a supposed kind. By the same token, it is no explanation of the many features common to all horses, say, to specify that horses all have some genetic material that determines manes, and some other genetic material that determines uncloven hooves, and some other genetic material that determines their head shape, and so on. We would not yet have explained why all these different genetic features are found together in horses. Equally, a constructivism that appeals to individual, collective and material representations may certainly explain *singular* generalizations or stabilities among members of human kinds, but taken in conjunction, they do not indicate a common cause (Godman, Mallozzi and Papineau, 2020).

## 3.4  Summary

Chapter 3 looked at various existing approaches to social categories and human kinds in the philosophical literature to identify their problems as well as their contributions in going forward with my own account. It has been a long chapter, so a brief summary is due.

I began with the *multiple-realization thesis* that takes human kinds to be distinctive from physical kinds because of their multiply realizability. I soon moved on to critically scrutinizing the functional thesis that often comes part and parcel with multiple realization but argued that, while it can explain single projectability, it fails to explain kinds' *multiple* projectability.

I then turned to the large social ontology literature that treats human kinds as social institutions and focuses on their so-called *status functions*, normative properties such as the rights or obligations that these groups might have. According to this literature, these properties are arrived at by *collective agreement* (John Searle) or by a *social equilibrium* (Francesco Guala). I did not find the debates in social ontology about how we arrive at status functions entirely convincing – and especially not the explanation of discoverable properties of human groups provided by Searle – but argued that the account raised pertinent issues about how existing power structures affect human kinds, which I return to in Chapter 7.

Finally, I turned to those that, like myself, have come to human kinds from the natural kind tradition. There is something to be learned from all of these accounts, and I will build on some of them in the following chapters. But in terms of finding a common cause, I argued that they are all found lacking. We can see this in a master argument or dilemma that arises in concert against accounts of kinds as characterized by causal homeostasis, looping or social construction.

Either:

1 The common-cause-mechanism is an *abstract* (homeostatic, similarity- or conformity-conducive) mechanism. In that case, however, we do not have a workable distinction between genuine kinds that support multiple projectability and categories which do not (i.e. *White horses*).

Or:

2 The common-cause mechanism is a *conjunction of different proximate mechanisms*. This looks like an explanation of single projections and stabilities across members, but *no* explanation of why the multiple projections *come together* in different instances of a kind.

The causal and HPC accounts of kinds is largely vulnerable to the first horn of the dilemma, as is a certain construal of looping effect account. Social constructivism, however, is more vulnerable to the second horn of the dilemma, as is another construal of looping effects.

It is entirely open to advocates of these positions to claim that they are simply not designed to address common-cause questions. This is fine. It just shows that if there is such an interest (which I hope to have convinced you of earlier in Chapter 2), then it is worth exploring another approach, which is what I turn to next.

## Notes

1 This section draws on material published in Godman (2015).
2 This is also the view of prominent critics of multiple realization such as Lawrence Shapiro and Thomas Polger, who agree with many advocates that the interesting issue is not the ubiquity of multiple realization: "The question of choosing between realization theories and identity (reductionist) theories should not be about counting up examples. . . . The amount of multiple realization in the world is important, but counting cases will not solve the dispute" (2016, p. 34).
3 Papineau also recognizes this limitation in the use of selection-based SS categories: "However, selection-based patterns might be argued to fall short of the requirements for a genuine 'science' in a different respect. Paradigm examples of natural kinds enter into lots of laws, not just single ones" (2010, p. 188).
4 It is much less clear, for instance, how ambitious the program for unification of social science is for those interested in institutions in terms of joint commitments (Gilbert, 2013) or the "we-mode" (Tuomela, 2010).

5 Even though I hint at generalizable features of an explanatory framework of collective intentionality that should spell trouble also for related accounts in social ontology, it is of course possible that other accounts will fare better than the ones I consider (for a useful catalogue of different options, see Epstein, 2018).

6 That is not to say that some discovered facts about groups cannot be exploited within society to achieve certain ends: the relative caring properties of women exploited in unpaid or poorly paid labor, or the relative aggression of men exploited in their recruitment for war and conflict. But here the function of these properties does not explain the facts to begin with; rather, a discoverable generalization is harnessed to certain functional ends.

7 I am grateful to Pekka Mäkelä for making this interesting suggestion.

8 A referee of this book has suggested that perhaps the relatively high rate of suicide among doctors is a case of such discoverable fallouts. Here the collective recognition of doctors means they have access to the relevant drugs, which is one candidate explanation for the higher rate of suicide among medics. But there are surely other plausible explanations of this generalization, such as the (relative) expectations they have of themselves, combined with high levels of work-life stress, for example.

9 The identity of the relevant collective and its members responsible for realizing the relevant recognition tend to be neglected – not only by Searle and Guala, but in social ontology in general, which makes ubiquitous use of notions of collective attitudes (see also Mäkelä & Ylikoski, 2003).

10 Since this exchange, both authors have been less interested in the question of how "natural" human kinds really are – as am I (basically because what is "natural" is at least as controversial as what natural kinds are) (see also Hacking, 2007b).

11 Thanks to a referee for making the commitments of pluralists more precise.

12 A second way in which Hacking's and Searle's accounts differ concerns the differential powers *different kinds of* collectives have over kinds. Expert endorsement and individuals who have been the target of classification tend in Hacking's case studies to have comparatively greater effects than, say, the collective of those who are disinterested in the kind in question.

13 As an anonymous referee points out, Hacking sometimes stresses the idea that looping effects are "motley" – if so, from this perspective, stable classification may not be possible.

14 When I discussed this phenomenon with my friend Sonja LaBianca, who is a clinical psychiatrist, she told me that she knew of a couple of wandering men in our neighborhood, Nørrebro in Copenhagen. We agreed it would be interesting to know if there have ever been any female wanderers, and if so, why they are (still) so under-represented.

15 Finally, some reasons for behavioral changes are neither strategic nor non-strategic, according to Mallon, but purely *automatic*, in that they bypass conscious awareness entirely. As an example, he mentions how even minimal group distinctions may cause individuals to act according to the in-group/out-group paradigm.

16 Mallon certainly acknowledges that self-undermining processes might occur, but his focus is on how human kinds are comprehensively explained by representational self-stabilizing processes.

17 This is just to give an example of how a constructivist account such as Mallon's might draw on a range of different explanatory resources to explain different properties of race and other human kinds. In fact, Mallon's and others' constructivism often wants to allow for more variation in these explanatory mechanisms.

# 4 Historical kinds

Consider a possible transformation of a by-now-familiar case. Suppose a group of white horses no longer simply share whiteness and other horsey features in common.[1] Suppose, for example, that these white horses also carry decorative saddles and harnesses, are all geographically isolated on a particular peninsula in the world by the name of Vitrosa and have developed a particularly strong preference for a local variety of fortified hay. I think we would begin to suspect that this group of white horses can support multiple empirical generalizations. That is, that there are probably further project-able features within the category than what meets the eye. What's more, we would be prone to ask our common-cause question: what explains the fact that these shared features come together in each instance of the group of white horses on Vitrosa?

In this scenario, I want to suggest that the common cause is *a common lineage of reproduction*. Suppose that for the group of white horses of Vitrosa, there is a shared lineage of reproduction among both horses and humans of a culture on the peninsula of Vitrosa. This culture has instigated a process by which all horses are modeled on a particular ancestral population of horses of this human culture (that were either bred by the human culture or were selected from diverse locations for their whiteness). The current members' historical relationship to this original group has allowed the descendant horses to share a cluster of features in addition to their whiteness: their geographic distribution, the food preferences and perhaps many more surprising cultural features attached to being raised and encultured in Vitrosa.

The white horses of Vitrosa are, in this case, a *historical* kind. The particular features of white horse may have different immediate explanations (the decorative saddles and harnesses are due to local craftsmanship; the uniform feeding of the fortified hay have shaped the feeding preferences; the geographical limitation is due to the coexistence with the particular cultural group of people and so on) but it is the shared history of reproduction that explains why all these features *correlate* in different instances. It is the relationship to a common model that is the common cause of the shared features of the white horses in Vitrosa.

Several authors have argued that species are historical kinds and considered some other cases which we might generalize to (Griffiths, 1999; Millikan, 1999, 2000; Bach, 2012). In my view, however, some far simpler cases can illustrate how a shared lineage from a common model becomes a common cause. Let us take Leo Tolstoy's *War and Peace*. Here are some instantiations of *War and Peace*: the paperback on my bookshelf with the front page torn off, the one in my local library, the recent BBC series and the superior Russian film version from 1969. All of these are members of the same historical kind as they are all copies of the same original version. The fact that they are copies also *explains* why certain reliable common features reoccur in different instances of the kinds: the main protagonist of *War and Peace* is Pierre; the central love story is the one between Natasha and Prince André; the setting is Russia during the early 19th century.

These properties correlate in each particular instance of the work, but they are certainly not explainable by any common eternal physical laws. The different copies are not even physically *alike*. They can be made of different kinds of paper, or of board, or written in Braille, and then there are audio versions on magnetic tape or digital disc. Rather, all these instances are members of the same kind because they are all copies of an original. Their shared features are all due to their being a result of a chain of copying. In this case, purely this chain of reproduction, not any common laws, explains the shared features.

Granted, in the case of literary categories the common properties are rather mundane. Scholars of literary and comparative studies may be far more interested in similarities and variations between *different* literary works: say, *War and Peace* on the hand and *Freedom* by Jonathan Franzen on the other. Yet, notice that even this kind of study would only make sense against a background of kind-identity between items. The claim here is that such kind-identity is provided by the historical chain of reproduction of a kind. Nor do the shared features of *War and Peace* constitute a trivial outcome. After all, they demand, among other things, the invention and successful execution of the printing press, well-maintained technologies and legal institutions to ensure common features among instances.

So how can we get a clearer sense of what the reproduction entails that may also apply more broadly to the case of human kinds? Here, inspired by the work of Peter Godfrey-Smith, is a basic outline of the conditions (2009, pp. 69–87).

A *reproductive lineage* among instances of a historical kind requires:

1 The existence of a model(s);
2 New member(s) produced in interaction with a model (or other past members);
3 The interaction with past models (or members) causes the new members to resemble past member(s); and
4 Steps 2–3 recur between members that are not models.[2]

Jointly, these conditions create historical kinds. Historical kinds are constituted by their process of reproduction. This account is compatible with the means and mechanisms of reproduction being extremely diverse, including, for example, type setting, copying machines, genetics, epigenetics and, particularly for human kinds, various modes of social learning. Many of these examples will be reviewed more closely in what follows.

Millikan notes that some kinds, such as artefacts, result from a template copied in *mass production*: "Items coming off of an assembly line are *not copied from one another* but originate from a single repeated process" (2017, p. 15f., emphasis added). But in cases of *reproduction* the process is different. Here, *past members*, not just the original models, ensure the production of new members and the *re*production of shared features (i.e. criteria 4).[3]

If one were to overlook the significance of the interaction between members being the cause of the similarity between them, one might think that historical kinds are even more ubiquitous but also uninteresting. Muhammad Khalidi gives the example of chemical kinds where we can cite historical explanations for new member occurrence. For example, most helium-4 in the universe is created by the past combination of two helium-3, a nuclei reaction that emits two protons (2013, p. 139). But kinds due to reproduction are historical in a much stronger sense. It is not merely that there can be or often is a causal contact with previous members, but that there *must be* – a new token member must be born of previous members or models (or in boundary cases, closely related ancestors and descendants). Without the chain or reproduction, there would simply be no new members and no shared properties.

Perhaps not all reproduction gives rise to historical kinds. The reproduction of single fleeting features, such as when a five-month-old baby happily reproduces the smile of her caregiver, might be one example. Lovely though these events are, the copies of a singular smile do not really form a kind with their originator – unless we for poetic purposes want to note the resemblance in curvature and form between the baby's smiles and those of its carer. Historical kinds, in contrast, have *multiple* shared features and typically also multiple stages of reproduction. Items like copied smiles share only a couple of features with their origin and are reproduced once or a couple of times. There will nevertheless be a continuum between the two, and the boundary is going to be blurry for some cases.[4]

Following this initial outline of what historical kinds are and how they come about, let's look in more detail at the general arguments for their having common-cause *explanations*. First, in Section 4.1, I investigate why a common cause of a historical kind *explains*. And then, in Section 4.2, I ask why one should suppose that the common cause of a historical kind can uniquely pick out a kind; in other words, how lineages *individuate* members of a kind.

## 4.1 Lineages as common-cause explanations[5]

Why, then, is a lineage or a chain of reproduction a *common-cause* explanation? What about this chain explains the correlations of properties shared between different instances? The appeal to lineages suggests we should look at two standard types of explanations discussed in evolutionary biology:

> (1) Why do certain phenotypic traits, e.g. $P_1$ of a species $S_1$, develop?
> (2) What led to there being a species $S_1$ (or Kind$_1$) with certain phenotypic traits $P_1$?

The first question is about the development or ontogeny of traits, and the second about the phylogeny or historical emergence of the traits. Ernst Mayr (1961) called these two questions "proximate" (1) and "ultimate" (2), respectively, while many prefer Philip Kitcher's (1984) terminology of "structural" (1) and "historical" (2) (see e.g. Devitt 2008, pp. 351–355). Notice that these questions are applicable not only to evolutionary biology but to all historical sciences where the original circumstances that brought about a property or a kind might be different from the current (proximate) explanation for its occurrence.

One could say that the common-cause question does answer the first proximate question (1), since it explains a *proximate fact*; namely, why contemporary instances all display a great number of common traits, $P_1$ . . . $P_n$. The historical common-cause explanation says that this is due to their all being copied from a common source. But the way proximate or structural explanations tend to be employed focuses on *singular traits* that are multiply instantiated, not *collections of traits* that are multiply instantiated.

Moreover, Kitcher's and Michael Devitt's use of the term "structural" for questions of the first type seems to prejudge the case against certain answers to such questions. This structural thinking seems to have its roots in the predominant model of kinds in chemistry (and perhaps physics) or what Millikan calls "eternal" kinds (1999, 2000),[6] where the shared properties are thought to be determined by internal composition and the universal and eternal laws of nature. Chemical substances perhaps remain the best paradigm of these kinds (see also Hendry, 2016; Weisberg et al., 2019, esp. section 4.5). Here, the set of laws consequent on the particular molecular composition of any given chemical substance, say sulphuric acid, would jointly constitute the common cause. The structural composition explains why samples share the same melting and boiling point, the same propensity to combine with other substances in fixed proportions, the same liquid density, electrical and thermal conductivity, and so on.

There is no need to quarrel with this type of common-cause explanation for some kinds; they are simply not fitted to most human kinds. But to the extent that "structural" or "proximate" entails an answer in terms of intrinsic composition rather than historical properties like those of a chain of reproduction, the terminology simply rules out the alternative historical option by fiat. I therefore think there is good reason *not* to assimilate common-cause explanations (that explicitly do not bias the answer) with structural and proximate explanations.

It is in fact more likely that the historical common-cause explanation gets mixed up with the ultimate or historical explanation of the second type (see e.g. Devitt, 2018). They really are completely distinct, however. Let us, again, consider *War and Peace*. The question of how or when Leo Tolstoy's ideas and production of the work emerged is distinct from the claim that subsequent instances are all *reproductions* of that original. The different instances of *War and Peace* share multiple features with one another *however* the original book came about. Or consider a request for an explanation of the properties common to Christianity. To answer this, we do not have to specify when Christianity started. Maybe we should date it from Jesus, or from the first Pope, or from the Council of Nicaea. But our historical account of the kind would seem to stand up perfectly well whichever event we use.

Others are concerned that historical common-cause explanations are insubstantial since lineages are only *relational* to their members (Okasha, 2002; Devitt, 2008). It is not quite clear what exactly these authors think is the problem with the relational aspect of an explanation but suppose one is asking for a manageable model of what these explanations should be. There are in fact several attempts in evolutionary biology underway to do exactly this. David Hull (1975), Eric Desjardins (2011) and Marc Ereshefsky (2012, 2014) argue that the historical relations of lineages explain via citing the particular lineage's *path dependency*. Path-dependent explanations do not merely relate to the initial causal state or origin of a kind (e.g. last common ancestor or source of novel adaptations etc.) but include *all* relevant causal factors and their order relevant to the explanandum (Ereshefsky, 2012, 2014).

Compare a lineage of a historical kind with that of a timeline. The timeline can be thought of as a useful representation of a purely temporal sequence of events. But it can also be misleading: temporally ordered events of a timeline need not have any particular causal relation with one another or with an overall outcome. In contrast, a lineage is useful not merely as it orders events temporally (and spatially); if it is correct, or approximately so, it also reveals a particular causal pathway of new members coming about and at the same time retaining projectable features with their ancestors. They do not come about through some pre-established harmony; the pattern comes about through a range of causally connected events.

For historical kinds there are also certain causes in the path of the kind that stand out. These are the causal interactions that forge reproductive bonds requisite for historical kinds. In the case of species, for example, it is the matter of proximate genetic mechanisms for the production of new members and their traits. Recent work in epigenetics and niche constriction theory suggests we should also go beyond the intrinsic properties of organisms. That is, some reproductive mechanisms are extrinsic (yet proximate) to the organism and can also contribute to the reproduction of many traits, either by being a condition for successful reproduction, reproducing traits on their own, or by weeding out deleterious mutations.[7] The lineage is therefore a *causal pathway* that is scientifically tractable – also in the human sciences, as we shall see.

The lineage to a common model also has the virtue of bestowing our common-cause explanation with *counterfactual force*. If there had been different causal factors and a different temporal or spatial order of events along the way, the lineage would also have been different, and different projectable properties would have been associated with it. In fact, historical explanations might seem maximally sensitive to counterfactual change. That is, had *any* part of history been different, the historical kind in question would also have been a different one from the one it actually is. However, though the historical pathway certainly confers a significant counterfactual force to the explanation, we must also keep the explanandum in mind; namely, the kind's particular cluster of projectable features. Not all things in the pathway are relevant for explaining this structure.[8]

So far, I have argued that historical path dependency qualifies as a *bona fide causal explanation*, but how come relations of reproduction to a common model also explain the property correlations associated with the kind more specifically? First, the initial models for historical kinds must have several correlated properties such that an interaction which reproduces their features will also lead to its descendants sharing similarly rich correlations of features.

But the existence of a model with a rich set of correlations is not sufficient to produce a kind either. If no successful copying process had been initiated, the rich set of features would not be instantiated in any new instances. So, these two features – the particular model with multiple correlated features *and* a successful reproductive chain – are then both necessary and sufficient for a common-cause explanation of a historical kind.

Notice that such a lineage is not merely similarity-conducive like Boyd's homeostatic mechanisms are. A reproductive connection to a model with a rich set of features warrants expectations that *multiple similarities* will come together in new instances of a historical kind. That is not to say that reproductive mechanisms are an all-or-nothing affair. In fact, the fecundity among instances can vary along both the dimensions of fidelity and multiplicity of features (as the earlier example of the baby's copied smile, on reflection, indicates). The reproductive connection with past models rich in features means that historical kinds are always conducive to the production of multiplicity rather than singularity, but just how many properties end up being produced will vary depending on both the model and the mechanisms for reproduction.

## 4.2 Humankind and Swampkinds: how lineages individuate

The notion of path dependency of the last section actually allows us to adopt two different perspectives on the lineages of historical kinds. The first one is the one we have focused on thus far: that of a token *causal process* that can explain. The flip side of this perspective is that of *individuating kinds* and *demarcating members of a kind*: the idea that a spatial-temporal pattern uniquely belongs to each historical kind. Path-dependency then means that there is a distinctive historical pathway that each historical kind has, in fact, taken.

The issue of individuation is part and parcel of addressing the common-cause question. To be precise, the common-cause question has two components: one to do with individuation and one to do with explanation. The explanation component is the one stressed and addressed explicitly so far: what is the causal explanation of different instances of a kind sharing a range of properties? But since the explanation should also be specific to all and only the instances or members of a kind, there is also an individuation or identity condition implied by the question.[9]

Individuation or demarcation of relevant kinds has also proved to be a big issue in the debate about the nature of species (Godman, 2019). We need to individuate species like we need to individuate kinds since we need a determinate way to assign individuals to the different species – and kinds – they belong to. Therefore, it is worthwhile thinking about whether a historical lineage can individuate in the case of species, such as in the case of humankind (or *Homo sapiens*) itself, so as to also inform the discussion of the human kinds. As we will see, the issue of individuation also has profound consequences for categorizing gender in the next chapter.

If a kind is a historical kind with a lineage to a common model as its common-cause explanation, it is then the historical relation of that lineage that individuates. The idea that we can individuate according to a historical relation to a common origin originates with Charles Darwin. As Stephen J. Gould writes: "Before the *Origin*, scientists had sought the intrinsic purpose and meaning of taxonomic order. Darwin replied that the ordering reflects historical pathways pure and simple" (1986, p. 60). This insight was carried through in the subsequent work in species classification within the Modern Synthesis, represented by figures such as Theodosius Dobzhansky, George Simpson and Ernst Mayr and the rise of phylogenetics. At least at first pass, the individuation criterion follows straightforwardly from this work: an organism belongs to a kind, say humans, in virtue of its spatio-temporal location in the tree of life. Then the unique historical relation of spatially and temporally ordered individuals unites its members in a lineage. The key here is to appreciate how the historical relation is a relation (or relational property) that an instance could not lose without also ceasing to be a member of that particular taxon or kind.

This criterion of individuation already helps us with a definitive answer to certain thought experiments. Imagine, for instance, that you are out walking in the Indian jungle and encounter something that looks like a tiger, moves like a tiger and roars like a tiger. You would certainly be justified in thinking that what you have encountered is, indeed, a tiger. But now also suppose that the individual in question has in fact due to some chemical miracle emerged from a nearby swamp as a stroke of lightning hit the earth. Would you still think this is a tiger we are dealing with?[10] On the historical-reproductive account, we will have to say, "no", this is an individual with the kind of history of a swamp tiger, or rather, *not* the kind of history shared by members of the kind tiger (*Panthera tigris*).

Notice that another result follows from this. Because the swamp tiger does not share a lineage of historical reproduction with tigers, we cannot make the same assumptions that we normally do when we meet one member of a kind, tiger, and use the information we acquired from encounters with other tigers. This is true no matter how many similarities are noted among "swamp tigers" and real members of the kind *Panthera tigris* (i.e. including genetic similarities). Just as in the case of the category *White horse*, we should not assume that they share further features beyond the ones that arose as a consequence of this freak accident. Recall that the whole point of there being common causes of similarities among instances is that it licenses expectations of further commonalities among members. In the case of the swamp tiger, we are imagining that no such common cause exists.

The case of the swamp species is also different from the successful case of cloning. Here the reproductive mechanisms involved in cloning technology, and so the nature of what facilitates the historical link might differ from the norm of "typical" reproduction. But it is nevertheless true that there is a real interaction between members that produces a rich cluster of resemblances (thereby fulfilling the conditions of reproduction stated earlier in this chapter). So, clones, unlike swamp individuals and their twin earth cousins, can certainly be members of historical kinds.

Both thought experiments and real experiments like clones can help set us straight with respect to our theoretical commitments. (You might, however, find my results counter-intuitive, but then I urge you to focus on some more substantial arguments for the epistemic virtues of historical kinds. I don't think intuitions on their own should be given much weight.) Historical lineages might all the same seem quite obscure to the naked eye. It is not as if we can simply *see* the lineage as a tail that trails behind each individual. Yet the human sciences should take comfort in the fact that we can arrive at methods for tracking these seemingly unobservable tails by the use of cladistics and phylogenetic methods for reconstructing lineages.

Phylogenies in biology are constructed based on different methods of producing data, either on morphological evidence or, more commonly, molecular evidence of DNA and RNA sequences. They map species in trees according to the principle where a greater number of traits and characters is taken as evidence of two species having more recent common ancestry compared to two species with fewer shared characters. The method assumes that convergent evolution, where analogous traits arise independently in lineages without common ancestry, is rare. Increasingly, computational phylogenetics – explicitly designed to not confirm pre-existing assumptions of phylogenetic relationships – is used as further support for hypotheses concerning branching relationships. (See also Sober (2015) for details on how phylogenetics can conform to common-cause type of explanations.)

Take the case of the critically endangered Christmas Island shrew, *Crocidura attenuata trichura*. To a casual observer, these tiny, beady-eyed, mole-like individuals look exactly like the North American shrew, but by triangulating evidence from different domains, we get a genealogical tree where the Australian shrew is, for instance, more closely related to the kangaroo than it is to the American shrew. This has consequences for the scope and structure of inferences we can make about the kinds. The more we know about an individual's spatio-temporal position in the tree of speciation (we may know the whole, a partial bit of the tree, or more commonly just the close ancestors and the descendants), the more we know about the nature and scope of which inferences are justified, including what conservation efforts might be deemed appropriate (Eldridge, Meek, & Johnson, 2014).

So far, the human sciences seem rather disinterested in the job of reconstructing lineages of their kinds. Exceptions are linguistics, anthropology and archaeology, where the spread of language and material culture has been documented using phylogenetic techniques (Holden, 2002; Tëmkin & Eldredge, 2007). In these cases, however, they are mostly interested in the history or transmission of a linguistic item or material kind, rather than of individuation *per se*. But the objective in biological phylogenetics often is to precisely approximate the *best ways* to individuate and group biological kinds such as species. Such a concern to find the best groupings and the right means of individuation should also be more central to the human sciences, as will become evident in the next two chapters on gender and cultural kinds.

For many philosophers, lineages are nevertheless disappointing for the job of demarcating membership in kinds. So before moving to *human* historical kinds, we need to briefly consider an influential concern among those philosophers of science who are dissatisfied with using lineages or other chains of reproduction as a way of individuating kinds. They worry that we need to have a way of determining *at what point* an ancestral population is formed or *when* a lineage cleaves off from its ancestors. And so, they think that a lineage or chain of reproduction on its own will not be able to mark out a kind from the one that immediately precedes it (or succeeds it). Michael Devitt continues to press this type of concern and thinks that (mostly) genetic essences must be added alongside shared historical relations for successful individuation (2008, 2010, 2018). Others have supposed that historical lineages need to be supplemented with some form of *origin* essentialism, according to which each taxon would then also have a particular origin that is essential to the kind (see e.g. Hull, 1978; Griffiths, 1999).

Are lineages uninformative without an intrinsic essence or an origin?[11] I'm inclined to say "no". Marc Ereshefsky has recently suggested that because speciation is path-dependent, adding the origin to a process is an unnecessary addition (2014). The historical relation itself demarcates a kind, as it gives us a specific *order and pathway of events*. Thus, according to Ereshefsky, it is in no need of additional components. After all, a new species or kind does not merely come about as a result of mutations for new adaptations (or through reproductive isolation), but through a *specific order and pathway of events*, such as the temporal order of mutations. If the order of mutations were reorganized, speciation might in fact not have occurred (Beatty, 2006). So according to Ereshefsky, it is rather the other way around: the whole idea of an origin or a starting point for a species demands that a historical pathway has already been underway:

If one looks at the branching event at the time it occurs, a species' identity is not determined (ontologically) because the existence of that species is not yet established. Further along the historical path of the branch, we can retrospectively say that the new species began at the branching event. . . . If we want to talk about a species' essence in a historical sense, then that essence must be a species' origin plus its unique path. But in that case, the notion of origin is redundant: the idea of a unique path assumes a starting point.

(2014, pp. 724–725)

I think this argument from Ereshefsky is compelling, and it also chimes with an argument in the last section. There I argued that citing the origin is also not going to be sufficient for a common cause; we also require a reproductive path or process from this model to have a historical kind. Indeed, building on Ereshefsky's argument, we might say that a certain path-dependent process is needed to say that the initial origin, individuals or items *are* models. Therefore, we do not need to supplement the particular lineage with a point specifying exactly who the first members of the *Homo sapiens* were or when and where they arose. The path itself determines membership in the kind and its origin.

It could even be, ontologically speaking, that there is no precise origin or a precise number of past members due to the inherent vagueness in both the branching and the path-dependent process. A corollary of this is that the aim of finding a precisely quantified set of generalizations over a historical kind, whether that kind be human or biological, might not mirror reality. Statistical relationships with precise quantities tend to disguise the fact that a precise number of members or strict boundaries between populations typically do not exist. But this does not mean that most individuals' membership in a historical lineage of a particular kind will *not* be a definite matter; it will. It is just that the boundaries *between* historical kinds is often vague, such as in the creation of a new ancestral population of a historical kind.

## 4.3 Summary

In this chapter I have wanted to demonstrate the basic feature of a historical kind – a kind produced because there are chains of reproduction from certain individuals that stand as models for other individuals. That chain of reproduction to common models is also the common cause of kinds, such as in the case of literary works and of species. New members of a particular historical kind both come about and share features with their ancestors because they are all part of the same chain of reproduction.

I thus turn to *human* kinds – first the case of gender, then to some religions and a broader range of cultural kinds and finally ethnicity – to show that historical lineages can be common causes here as well. Only now it is because our culture can create lineages of its own.

## Notes

1　Thanks to Uskali Mäki for the inspiration for this thought experiment.

2　It occurs to me that there might be reasons to separate the concept of lineages from chains of reproduction depending on how much *lateral* reproduction (events of reproduction that occurs between individuals of different lineages) one allows there to be as part of a lineage. Yet cultural lineages surely must allow for some of this without lineages thereby merging. From now on I will treat these concepts mostly synonymously and hopefully this will not matter particularly to the discussion in this book. (See also Section 6.1's discussion on bacteria and the species template.)

3　Arguably, literary works like *War and Peace* seems to fall somewhere in between mass production and reproduction.

4　Some linguists may be interested in tracing the particular lineage of a particular sign or a particular word, reproduced multiple times, but with few shared features. Thanks to a reviewer of this book for the example.

5　The following two sections draw on material published in Godman (2018a) and Godman and Papineau (2020).

6　As Michael Devitt has pointed out, the term "eternal" is less than ideal for kinds in chemistry (personal correspondence). The members of Millikan's eternal kinds can be short-lived and in constant flux, such as when chemical substances and compounds undergo chemical reactions. Historical kinds, such as higher taxa, can, on the other hand, be very long-lived. Nor is the distinction best made at the basis of different scientific domains: the historical vs. eternal sciences (Millikan, 1999). That is because even some human kinds such as genetic disorders like Huntington's disease and some infectious diseases can be both historical kinds *and* be determined by universal Mendelian laws. But David Papineau and I argue that this kind of overdetermination of common causes is more the exception than the rule (2020).

7　As we saw in already Chapter 3, a *conjunction* of proximate reproductive mechanisms cannot be a rival common cause. Nor has the explanatory buck been passed to the more proximate features of the organisms; when we look to the mechanisms that explain reproduction, the explanandum in this case has simply changed.

8　Not all events will therefore affect the kind's distinctive inductive structure and need to figure in the explanans. Some relatively minor events in the course of the lineage will be included in the path of a species kind, such as an organism's retention of a novel mutation in response to a changing niche; other events, such as, presumably, some stillbirths, may have no bearing on the overall multiple projectability of the species and so can safely be excluded from the explanans. Equally, the relevant multiple projectability can subsume traits that are not unique to the kind (say they were also present prior to the evolution of a particular species), but the path-dependent explanation will then not include the emergence of such traits, but only their retention within the lineage.

9 For further discussion of the individuation and explanatory criteria and their relation see Godman (2018a).

10 In case any Swedish-speaking readers are interested, I have a shorter piece on this thought experiment, its origin in Donald Davison's thought and its relation to historical kinds (Godman, 2016a).

11 For an argument that the historical-reproductive account of species is not only independent of but also *superior* to Devitt's intrinsic essentialism, see Godman and Papineau (2020) and Godman et al. (2020).

# 5    Gender as a historical kind
## A plea for reclassification[1]

In this chapter I have two aims. I want to investigate whether gender is a historical kind due to cultural reproduction. I also want to back up a central claim championed in the work of Elizabeth Spelman (1988) and others, who have criticized a very universalist understanding of binary gender categories. I hope to show how a focus on particular cultural systems and models of gender can further support Spelman's claim. But this will lead to some fundamental rethinking of gender.

## 5.1 Gender models and social learning

One's gender is a rich category to belong to or identify with. It cuts across a wide variety of dimensions. Personal characteristics, clothing and bodily aesthetics, work and relationship roles are all marked in a gendered manner. As such, gender is an extremely potent category for structuring social life. As social psychologists have thoroughly documented, we are so used to gender pronouns, stereotyping and so on that we are almost blind to how pervasive it is (Liben & Bigler, 2017).

But the use of both gender generics and generalizations effectively disguise the fact that they are false for many, if not the majority of, individuals they are presumed to concern. Most significantly, what is gendered as belonging to men (or boys) and what is gendered as belonging to women (or girls) varies considerably across both time and cultures. In fact, variation within each gender category seems almost as compelling as the kind's inductive richness. This is true even for core characteristics of gender. Women serve as combat troops and game hunters in some non-industrial societies, for example, and in some hunter-gatherer societies fathers show intensive care for infants (Wood, Eagly, & Eisenberg, 2002).

So, there seems to be a lot of possible projections (and expectations!) based on belonging to a gender category while there is great variability across both time and space. The question I want to address in this chapter is, therefore, can we make sense of gender as a historical kind and thereby resolve this tension? I will argue that we can, but only if we are prepared to rethink our current gender categories of women and men.

First thing's first. One might think that any of the reliability of a gender category comes down to characteristics based on sex, i.e. our biology. The problem is that it is not just gender that is a tricky category; as has become increasingly obvious, so is sex. The binary sex distinction has come under fire in recent decades, as people have questioned whether there really are distinct biological (hormonal or genetic) causes of binary sex categories (see Blackless et al., 2000).

But even if there are some sex-based differences (and it is unclear both how binary and how reliable these differences are), most agree that these genetic, hormonal differences will in no way explain the range of gendered properties we are interested in within the human sciences: learned behavior, work and relationship roles. That is also not to say that there is not a strong relationship between sex and gender, especially since, as social psychologist Sandra Bem and others have argued, the perceived binary sex differences are coded into, or strongly associated with, two predominant *gender* categories: men (or boys) and women (or girls) These are the "lenses" through which we approach and regiment gender (1993). So, biological sexual categories and our perceptions of them will remain relevant in terms of explaining gender. In particular I think it is quite plausible that real, or at the very least perceived, physical sex differences played an important role in the original emergence of gender models (Wood & Eagly, 2012).[2]

But if gender is mostly due to culture rather than biology, how does the historical kind model work in this case? How can the interaction between different individuals occur such that new members of a gender come to resemble models (or their immediate predecessors)? Clearly the type of *template* or blueprint copying, exemplified by genetic transmission or copying machines, will not do. We simply need a richer sense of the mechanisms responsible for reproduction in the case of culture.

Theodore Bach (2012) has also argued that gender is a historical kind, and he has helpfully listed a number of causally interconnected components of a binary gender system that could be considered part of the machinery of reproduction of gender and gendered traits. These components include: binary sexual categories; conceptual gender dualism (including stereotypes and psychological essentialist bias); gender norms (moral disapproval of individuals' deviation from, and the moral approval of, conformity to gender norms); gender roles and identity; binary gender-socialization practices; certain social and legal institutions; and binary gendered artefacts (pp. 247–248).

This is a wealth of vehicles for reproduction, and without neglecting the importance of any of these aspects, it seems to me that they nevertheless leave aside the most interesting issue of social learning; namely, why do individuals learn from or copy certain models of gender or a perceived sex (and, as a result, acquire a hoard of resemblances)?[3] In short, why is the cultural reproduction of gender so potent?

At a basic level we can say that historical kinds exist in biology because, to inherit naturally selected traits advantageous to the individual organism, we need genetic and non-genetic biological (epigenetic) reproductive mechanisms as well as stable niches. In culture, historical kinds at first glance seem to exist because of the importance of passing on certain traits between kin and others within our group. But that is not the whole story. We social individuals are tuned to not only learn from (certain) others, but also *be* like (certain) others. As developmental psychologist Ina Užgiris has made clear we *re*-produce what others have in their turn produced and reproduced because it allows us to acquire useful skills and also to connect with others and belong to a group (1981).

But why is learning from and being of a category of gender, specifically, so important to many? As I see it, there are two plausible sets of reasons suggested in the literature on gender: *a deep sense of identification* or belonging that motivates one to be of a gender, and *the imposition of external socializing forces* that compel individuals to become of a gender.

The first set of motivations is primarily studied in the literature on gender identity. In fact, Wendy Wood and Alice Eagly (2015) make a useful distinction between two different traditions within gender identity research: one that measures the degree to which an individual identifies with gendered *traits* (often coded in terms of masculinity and femininity) and one that measures the degree to which an individual identifies as a *member* of a gendered group. According to the former tradition, gender identity could be thought of as a judgment about, or recognition of, how similar one is to certain gendered stereotypes in terms of the traditional division of labor roles, for example. The latter tradition broadly aligns with the theory of social identity in social psychology. Here the motivation for "self-categorizing" in terms of a gender is that it allows certain in-group ascriptions and at the same time allows distance from certain out-groups (Hogg & Turner, 1985). Thus, according to gender identity literature, individuals pick their models because of the sense of in-group belonging, or simply due to their perceived similarity with others.

Very often, though, gender identity and gender identification is also something imposed on the individual by external social pressures. This may happen through the desire to abide by (gender) norms to attain social approval, or indeed from a fear of disapproval or punishment if one were not to conform to the norms of the perceived sex or gender (see also Castro, Castro-Nogueira, Castro-Nogueira, & Toro, 2010). Although it is common wisdom in this literature that one learns more from some individuals than from others (e.g. Henrich & McElreath, 2003), this still leaves us with the question of why *gender* models, in particular, are so much more powerful than other culturally available models of social reproduction and learning (such as hair and eye color).

Perhaps part of the answer lies in the intensive and extensive role that gender plays in many areas of life that are likely to matter to the individual. This would fit best with the motivations described by gender identity research. Or perhaps, as the cultural evolution tradition instead tends to stress, it lies in the degree to which society tends to reward conformity with one's gender and to disapprove of gender or sex deviation. At any rate, the external pressures to conform and internal motivation to be alike and belong are not mutually exclusive and may both play a part in the explanation of why gender seems to matter and become a historical kind.

This might also seem like a way for the historical account of gender to reconcile the variation and the multitude of features belonging to a gender category. At least when it comes to *variation over time*, this seems right. If a person's gender is a result of accepted cultural reproduction from a chain of previous models, then each binary gender category may still display variation and change over time. Although each member of a gender is reproduced within a historical lineage that traces back to certain original models of gender, the lineage need not sustain all or even most properties originally associated with these models. At the same time, the lineages are maintained insofar as whenever a branch of gender (say, man) undergoes change, a relevant contrast is maintained between that and a different lineage (say, woman). In other words, as long as neither gender becomes extinct (that is, a category of a gender refers to an empty set), significantly branches off from a lineage or merges with another, we can have variation over time coupled with there being many, many features to be generalized about a gender.

But I think this conclusion is arrived at too hastily. It does not speak to the considerable variation of how gender is expressed in different cultures *at a single time*. That is because the claim so far has been about how variation can be retained *within* lineages. But what if there are more than two models of gender to begin with?

## 5.2 Beyond binary cultural systems of gender

I have shown just how contingent a system of gender is on two features of reproduction: a cultural niche with certain gender models and the motivations and pressures for gender-based social learning. I have also shown how we should expect that cultural reproduction within a lineage leads to change over time in the characteristics associated with a gender.

But there can also be more dramatic changes to a system of gender lineages. The original gender models might not have been binary to begin with; perhaps there were three or more gender models. Even supposing that we start out with a binary set of gender models (perhaps closely inspired by the perception of a binary sex), the reproduction can unfold such that it ceases to be binary. First, the binary lineages might merge at some point, or one or both genders might cease to exist.[4] Second, new alternative gender models may emerge either because an existing lineage has locally branched off into one or more new gender lineages. Third, relatedly, two lineages might partially merge such that we have three models.

Are any of these scenarios realistic? With respect to the first alternative, genderless cultural systems seem as rare as those in which gendered social learning does not occur (and perhaps for the same reasons). Although many individuals certainly identify in ways that cut across gender and perceived sex,[5] it is hard to find cultural systems that do not have *any* models of gender or have departed entirely from gender-based social learning. One almost has to go to science fiction to find some examples. Ursula Le Guin's *The Left Hand of Darkness* (2012) describes a society in which humans are not thought of or classified according to gender but are effectively genderless androgynes most of the time. But the sex of these individuals is also indeterminate, since in their fertile periods (kemmer) these individuals adopt either the female or the male sex.

The other options – where categories of gender have always been, or have become, non-binary – have, on the other hand, featured in multiple cultural systems. One of the longest-lasting alternative "genders" to achieve stability is the male *hijra* in Pakistan and certain parts of India dating back to the 16th century (Nanda, 1990). Another is the different varieties of *two-spirits*, documented in 130 North American tribes with both males and females having assumed alternative gender roles (Roscoe, 1993, p. 5). Anthropologist Will Roscoe documented the life of a particular two-spirit (referred to by Roscoe as the potentially offensive "berdache") in the late 19th century, We'wha, who lived among an isolated Zuni tribe near the New Mexico–Arizona border. In response to the question of how one should make sense of the We'wha's gender, Roscoe explicitly states that it is a matter of a third gender within the Zuni tribe:

> The answer to the question "Was We'wha a man or a woman?" is "Neither". That is, the sequence of initiations and social experiences that served to "cook" berdaches did not correspond to the sequence by which either men or women were "cooked". We'wha represented a third possibility in the Zuni organization and representation of gender – a third gender status.
>
> (ibid., p. 145)

I would contend that these type of alternative or third genders should be considered historical kinds of gender in their own right. A new model (or in the case of more than three genders, several models) has been introduced and reproduced in accordance with the process of gendered social learning described in the last section. Roscoe suggests that in the case of the third-gender status (or Ihamanaye) of We'wha, there are two main arguments for stabilized reproduction. First, as noted in the prior quotation, belonging to any gender in the Zuni tribe is part of a formalized process of cultural reproduction. In particular, it is a matter of ceremonial initiation rites in which a person passes from the genderless "uncooked" to the "cooked" stage of belonging to one of at least three genders and becomes versed in accompanying learned practices such as dress and mastered craftsmanship – especially pottery for the Zuni two-spirit (ibid., p. 123ff.). These practices serve to "scaffold" the reproduction between past models and new members of a particular gender. Second, the Zuni third gender is an attractive model of social learning in that two-spirits in the Zuni and in other North American tribes have occupied prestigious positions on many levels of their society – from being integrated into the origin myths to taking an active role in societal governance (ibid., p. 147ff.).

The hypothesis is that third or alternative genders are historical kinds in their own right with distinct common causes, and culture-specific norms and models of being of a gender sustain the kinds. Once the cultural system perishes, so does the life-support system for such genders (as, sadly, is largely the case with the third gender of the Zuni tribe).

But the examples of cultures in which gender is not a strictly binary concept do not merely demonstrate the contingency of the Western dominant binary cultural gender system. They also raise the question of what the actual common causes of our current kinds of gender are.

Since human populations all came from common ancestral groups, perhaps there were originally two binary models of gender. Alice Eagly and Wendy Wood (2005) have, for instance, suggested that the physical differences between the sexes – such as pregnancy and lactation among women and the greater size, speed and upper-body strength among men – gave rise to the original gender differences. In their account, this led men to perform tasks that required upper-body strength for extended periods of time uninterrupted by having babies. I think it quite plausible that some real, or at the very least perceived, physical sex differences played an important role in the original emergence of gender models.

But even if this shared perception of anatomy forms the basis of common binary models of gender in some or many cultures, it is not automatically retained over time. In particular, it does not bar the emergence of different gender systems, including different models of gender – binary and non-binary – in different cultures. The examples of the Zuni and other North American tribes show how likely it is that different, often relatively isolated, cultures have developed different interpretations of anatomy and sex and its meaning and also different models of gender. If this is so, why should we think that all who are treated as intuitively falling under the gender categories of "man" and "woman" have their respective common causes? Is it not more likely that different cultures have evolved their own binary or non-binary systems of gender where each system contains both qualitatively and numerically different historical kinds of gender?[6]

This clearly has consequences for the classification gender. It is not merely that the expression of gender changes over time and places; it is that without the assumption of cross-cultural common models that ground each category "man" and "woman", there simply is no historical chain uniting all individuals categorized as "women" and all those categorized as "men". True, one could still say that each individual "woman" is modeled from a gender variant within *some* cultural system of gender. But since many cultural systems have evolved their own gender categories, some of which are binary while others are not, one is not entitled to assume that each of these individuals classified as women will share a common cause with one another. In short, not all of those we think of as women presently and historically are members of the same historical kind of gender.

## 5.3  Why there is no easy fix via shared functions

Millikan suggest that some cross-cultural human categories might be down to our common psychological dispositions:

> [I]n so far as social scientists sometimes generalize across radically different cultures, not just, say, across Western cultures, the common historical thread in studying kinds of social groups is mainly just human psychology, the common psychological dispositions of the historical species Homo sapiens.
>
> (1999, p. 57)

Since we humans have broadly the same psychological goals and learning strategies built into us, Millikan reasons that we can explain the success of some broad cross-cultural categories that are historical kinds not via social learning but via our functional psychology (1999, p. 63). Her examples are certain economic systems that re-emerge in different cultures. Others might be certain rituals at the beginning of life and death that occur independently in different cultures because they fulfill a vital need that has a common human origin.

Perhaps some human categories are inevitable due to how deeply they are embedded in our common human psychology or learning strategies, but gender is unlikely to be one of them. That is because gender both can be, and as we saw in the last section, indeed *has* been modeled in several different ways in different cultures. There also seems to be no constraints on our basic learning mechanisms or our vital needs that mean we *have to* end up with binary gender categories.

Bach suggests we can nonetheless retain the kindhood of cross-cultural categories such as "woman" and "man" due to *convergent evolution* across culture (2012). On this view, some categories are not united by any shared history, not even at the basic psychological level. What unites the categories is their shared teleological function. Can teleology explain why generalizations about say, "women", can hold across time and place?

A typical case of a trait due to convergent evolution is the wing, which occurs in a variety of animals such as birds, bats and insects that, in contrast to homologous traits, lack a continuity with a common ancestor. Instead, these wings can be categorized together for having been selected to serve the *same teleological function* in the distinct species. So, whereas for Millikan cross-cultural kinds are homologues due to common origins of our human psychology, Bach considers gender to be a trait like the wing that has the same teleological function in different cultures. By teleological he means that the function is not only present across cultures; it is teleological since the *reason* these gender traits are reproduced in the different cultural systems lies in their past selected roles (ibid., p. 244 ff.). Teleology demands that the favorable effect of gendered traits within a cultural gender system *in the past* is what causes descendants of that culture to continue to possess them.[7]

I think this proposal is faulty in two respects. I have already argued that a selected function, on its own, *is not a common cause*; although it may explain single generalizations, a teleological function cannot explain why many, many shared features come together in an instance (see Section 3.1). In short, selected functions do not give rise to genuine kinds. But even if you are not persuaded of this general argument about kinds, I think there are additional reasons to be skeptical that this teleological strategy works in the case of a cross-cultural gender category.

In Bach's view, an individual may possess membership in both a historical kind of gender related to her particular culture *as well as* membership in a teleofunctional kind – the latter being a kind with an analogous cultural function to other members. Consequently, individuals descended from different historical models of gender may still share membership in virtue of the teleological function. One can therefore speak of sameness in teleological functioning across different gender lineages as well as sameness in the *breakdown* of the function. Bach gives the following example:

> American and Japanese women are not members of numerically the same historical kind. However, the historical gender roles in each

system are analogous. On account of their shared type of history, then, American and Japanese women are members of numerically the same teleofunctional gender kind. This means that both American and Japanese women can fail to satisfy their teleofunctional gender norm and yet both are still members in the cross-cultural teleofunctional gender kind (and, of course, they are still also members in their respective historical kinds).

(ibid., p. 262)

According to Bach's proposal, it may be possible to hold on to two cross-cultural categories of gender, "woman" and "man", due to shared teleological function. For instance, common selection pressures may lead women to be barred from certain leadership roles in different gender lineages, which is then attributed to a common teleofunctional role among all historical kinds of women. Or, common selection pressures may lead men to abuse their power for their sexual advantage in different lineages, and this explains a common teleofunctional kind: men.

But I worry about the science and epistemology of cultural teleological functions. How are we to ascertain the selection or selection pressure in these examples? If the teleological function is not to be merely a nominal status, there must be some way of *knowing* which features should form the basis of a teleofunctional kind. Even supposing that these cross-cultural generalizations are valid (which I think is dubious), is there really also the same cross-cultural *teleological or functional explanation* for why traits such as submissiveness and abusiveness re-occur in different cultures and lineages? This seems trickier to establish than is apparent at first glance. First, it seems plausible that it would take a relatively long time for a gender trait to acquire a teleological function – even within a single culture. Conversely, over large chunks of time and space, many cultural selective pressures on gender are bound to vary both within and between lineages. How do we then ground the supposed common tendency to abuse power for sexual advantage among contemporary middle-class men in Finland and contemporary working-class men in the Philippines, as well as between male aristocrats in either of these locations 300 years ago? Even accepting such a common tendency (true generalizations), the existence of common teleological roles among lineages is a different matter.

In truth, my worry about appealing to convergent cultural evolution here is an instance of the more general worry about the tendency to prioritize adaptationist hypotheses in evolutionary theorizing and to dismiss alternative causal explanations as simply "null hypotheses" (Lloyd, 2015). As Richard Lewontin and Stephen J. Gould have drawn our attention to, not all traits and products of biological evolution are due to selection; some arise via drift or by being "spandrels" – i.e. byproducts of other adaptations (1979). In the case of the evolution of culture, there are also several alternatives to adaptationist hypotheses. Some traits related to gender have simply developed as a result of individual trial-and-error learning. And when we are dealing with analogous traits that occur in *different* lineages, the alternative explanations multiply for each instance of the alleged "same" trait. For example, in the case of submissiveness: why could it not, for example, be social learning from a model in some cases that accounts for the trait, but individual learning in others?

Bach is right in highlighting how analogous social norms and beliefs about gender hierarchies, divisions of labor and sexual roles recur in distinct lineages. However, whether these beliefs and norms are shared between cultures to the extent that they generate meaningful teleological roles between lineages – thereby constituting teleological gender kinds – is another matter. I would make a much more modest claim, namely, that social norms and beliefs play a part in regimenting the reproduction of gender in a binary and non-binary manner in diverse lineages. I think this modesty is appealing in the historical kind model – an account that is inherently wary of sweeping generalizations across time and space. If the lineage of common descent is the common cause for why clusters of gendered traits come together in each individual of a gender kind, we need not suppose that a property such as submissiveness has a common explanation in different lineages (let alone a common explanation within the *same* lineage over time).

My current diagnosis is then that we should not attempt to "fix" the problem of cultural variation of gender via evoking cultural selection. I propose sticking to gender as a historical kind but, contra Bach, I also believe we would do well to divorce the historical kind hypotheses from any (cultural) adaptationist or teleological commitments. In the case of gender, this means that any reference to a gender is always a reference to a particular historical kind with common ancestry within a specific culture. The spatial-temporal proximity in reproduction guides the right individuation of kinds.

This still allows for a sense of gender identification (and imposition) within a historical lineage to trigger a sense of solidarity between different cultures. And some social learning can of course transcend a culture and a specific lineage. Let us say, for example, that injustices such as silencing and harassment take place within the lineage ($A_1$) in one cultural niche (A), and that this fosters identification with a similarly unjustly treated gender from a different lineage ($B_1$) within a different cultural niche (B).[8] The likely result is that there will be cultural transmission between the different lineages $A_1$ and $B_1$ – not least in how to develop strategies to deal with and overcome these injustices.

Values of solidarity and concern for others may then bridge different cultures, and this can help promote partial convergence of both models and gender lineages. When this solidarity and concern crosses cultures, this can also lead to the convergence of new gender models that are both popular and progressive (perhaps devoid of hierarchical thinking). In fact, the convergence of new models of gender is probably more likely given the prevalence of social media, the Internet and travel that harness existing tendencies of gendered social learning (and sometimes without needing the mediation of solidarity). Lateral cultural transmission is thus likely to extend the scope of membership in a historical kind of gender somewhat by merging different gender systems, particularly during the past couple of generations.

Nevertheless, there will be many, especially historical, cases of individuals where such lateral transmission is not only insignificant, but even impossible. But of course, these individuals still belong to a lineage within *some* gender system. Thus, as in the case of convergent evolution, we should not put our faith in lateral transmission for generating cross-cultural gender kinds. (For what it is worth, I therefore believe that thinking of the partial convergence within these different gender systems in terms of coalitions and alliances between historically constrained memberships rather than in terms of common membership.)

## 5.4  Summary

In sum, the variation of gender display that occurs within a culture can be reconciled with the kind still displaying an ample amount of culturally inherited attributes if we think of gender categories as cultural historical kinds. But there is a limit to how much variation within a kind we can accept as the guiding principle is still reproduction from common origins. If there is no reproductive link (i.e. social learning) between different cultures, we will not have sameness in kind and should rethink cross-cultural gender classifications.

More positively, an account stating that gender is a historical kind makes sense of why claims about gender are typically more plausible if they are more narrowly indexed – or, in the terms of the account, indexed to specific lineages of reproduction. In other words, both political agendas and social science should respect the particular cultural niche in which gender is reproduced and should be cautious in making sweeping cross-temporal and cross-cultural claims. It thus seems that we are at least *prima facie* correct in being skeptical of many far-reaching gender generalizations, given that in many cases there may rightly be nothing uniting the group represented in the subject in the first place!

# Notes

1 This chapter draws on material published in Godman (2018b).
2 Nevertheless, it should be born in mind that not all cultures assume a close connection between sex and gender, as we will soon see.
3 I write gender or sex as we are often not aware of a distinction, and in many cases it does not matter. Even just a perception of a minimal biological marker is sufficient for identifying a model for learning or to be a target for instruction. Thanks to Sally Haslanger for making this more salient to me.
4 I am inclined to think that the possibility of the two genders merging into a single gender and one or two genders becoming extinct, for most practical purposes, amounts to similar scenarios.
5 Depending on the details of the case, these individuals would, according to the historical account, belong to both genders or neither gender (and thereby also stand as a possible model for a new gender).
6 There is also a significant debate these days about the genderqueer category that not only opposes the Western binary gender divide but where individuals tend to reject any gender or sex belonging *at all*. In this case it is debatable whether there is enough social learning present among individuals belonging to the category to postulate genderqueer as a historical kind (and so it is also questionable if there is any multiple projectability among members) (e.g. Dembroff, 2020).
7 Although it is not clear whether he has in mind cultural group selection or if it is also an advantage to the individual trait bearer's reproductive fitness.
8 See Shelby (2007) for a developed statement concerning social-cultural links of solidarity in notions of race.

# 6 What is culture and how is it realized?

In this chapter I want to think more broadly about the kinds that are a result of cultural reproduction. It is not just kinds of people, like kinds of gender, that can emerge from cultural reproduction, but also other forms of culture such as certain religions, political ideologies, musical genres and other ways of life. In many of these cases, the instances are not individual human beings as in the case of gender kinds (what many refer to as *proper* kind members), but the members are represented by different instances in time (often referred to as *time-slices*). I will argue that a historical kind framework also helps establish the right principles for what questions to ask about these cultural kinds. I will also return to the question of multiple realization and argue that there is a very plausible case for multiple realization of such cultural kinds.

## 6.1 Historical kinds as higher kinds

Just as members of a kind share multiple but not innumerable properties, there also constraints on what *type of properties* and what *type of questions* you can ask about a kind. Consider the questions that are meaningful to ask about a kind, such as mercury: "What is the boiling point of *mercury*?" (356.7°C); "What is the freezing point of *mercury*?" (−38.8°C); "What is the molecular weight of *mercury*?" (200.6). Now compare this with the questions that we can pose about cats, such as "What do *cats* eat?"; "How should one hold a frightened *cat*?"; and "How does the anatomy of a *cat* assist it to orient itself as it falls so that it lands on its feet?" The questions we ask about mercury are not meaningfully asked about cats and *vice versa*. There are real constraints to what *type of questions* we might want to pose about a kind. As Millikan puts it succinctly: "You can ask how tall Mama is, but not how tall gold is" (2000, p. 9).[1]

So how do we know what *type* of questions one might ask, and what *type* of generalizations one might make about a kind? This is where we need to climb up our inductive ladder. Individuals fall into kinds and kinds in their turn fall into what Millikan calls "higher kinds". A higher kind gives us a *template*, or a cognitive guide, for what questions will be relevant to ask about the kinds that fall under it.[2] The category of *Vertebrates* corresponds to a higher kind. We can ask questions about the morphology, anatomy, physiology, diet and reproductive behavior of any given vertebrate species. But it will not be meaningful to pose questions about the injuries or learned behaviors of any given vertebrate. The particular morphology, anatomy and so on of any one vertebrate, such as domesticated house cats, will be different from that of other vertebrates. Still, the different vertebrate species will all coincide in the distinctive set of questions that might be posed about each and all of them.

Evidence from developmental psychology suggests that the discovery of such higher kinds is typically much more cognitively demanding than the discovery of more basic kinds. Infants recognize and identify cats before they recognize animal species, or armchairs before they recognize furniture, for example. Still, this ability to perform something akin to a "meta-induction" over the basic kind's properties also arises relatively early in our first years of life (see e.g. Mandler & McDonough, 1998).

Knowing the hierarchical structure of kinds is especially important for individuals and kinds you have not yet encountered. We may have lived all our life without encountering and hearing about the African dormouse, but presumably we would still have encountered plenty of other mammals to have a template of a relevant higher kind (mammal or vertebrate species), and therefore know what sort of questions are relevant to ask (Millikan, 1998, p. 65).

How about higher kinds of human kinds? I would suggest that we might add the different cultural systems of gender of the last chapter (i.e. Japanese gender system, Nordic gender system) to the list of higher kinds. For each of these higher kinds, we can also develop templates for the relevant questions to ask about their respective kinds. Abrahamic religion strikes me as another higher kind composed of Islam, Christianity, Judaism and several other Abrahamic religions. It supports questions for each of the religions that fall under it, such as: What is the significance of the patriarch Abraham in the religious practice?; What are the sacred texts?; What is the status of Jerusalem? and so on. The questions are meaningful to each kind, but will have different answers for each Abrahamic religion. They will not be as meaningfully posed about another kind we will consider shortly, *Buddhism* (nor are they meaningfully posed of all monotheistic religions).

The importance of such higher kinds, also in the human sciences, is then that they can guide inquiry into the kinds that fall under them, including those we have not encountered earlier. But Millikan seems to object to this application of her theory of higher kinds because of her skepticism of the possibility that many historical kinds, arguably especially human kinds, can be organized into the hierarchical structures of higher kinds.

> Relatively few historical kinds furnish subject matter for science, however, partly because relatively few (unlike animal species and chemical kinds) fall neatly into higher kinds that furnish general *a posteriori* principles of induction. Relatively few are such that one can tell in advance details about which determinables can be projected over the kind.
>
> (Millikan, 1999, p. 56)

In response, recall first that I have argued in Chapter 2 that many of the generalizations that we are concerned with in the human sciences are more about a comparative tendency *between* groups than about a strong regularity *within* a group. Now we are in a position to see that, in fact, comparisons of different groups along dimensions of gender, sexuality or ethnicity presupposes that they fall into higher kinds to which the same questions might be posed. Otherwise, one could easily be charged with comparing "apples and oranges" – groups where no comparison is relevant (although as an aside comparing apples and oranges along the dimension of being a fruit strikes me as perfectly plausible).

Millikan also seems to demand too much of higher kinds in general in this quote. If higher kinds must provide only well-focused templates with carefully defined hierarchical rules, then we will in fact run into trouble with Millikan's own example of animal species. A historical account of the species category (including the animal species category) has come under pressure lately precisely because people worry whether they exclude some intuitive species. One common example is prokaryotes such as various forms of bacteria that do not seem to form real lineages because of their pervasive lateral transmission, i.e. reproduction that seems to undermine the formation of lineages (see e.g. Doolittle, 1999). Does this mean that prokaryotes are not species or that the account of species as a historical kind is mistaken? It seems to me that there is a third alternative, namely that the higher category, *Species*, is not perfectly well-focused with respect to the kinds that it is comprised of. Typically, we can ask about the lineage of a species, but not always; sometimes it will be something else responsible for the species' reproductive cohesion (see also LaPorte, 2017). My point is not to defend this third view; rather, it is to say that a well-focused template of a higher kind might be too demanding criteria for epistemic and scientific usefulness. Templates of species can be very useful as a cognitive guide to biological inquiry, despite not being perfectly focused.

Armed with templates of cultural *historical* kinds, they suggest a common set of meaningful questions about the spatial-temporal *lifespan* of their kinds such as, When did the particular religious practice *emerge* and where?; Where and by what means did a particular political ideology *spread* to new geographical areas?; At what period of time and where did a particular culinary art *change*?; When and where did a particular musical genre *die out*? Templates of historical kinds also yield further advantages. We can assume that the identity as well as some projectable stability is also *maintained* over time – the questions we should pose are more about *which* properties are maintained and which have changes or are prone to change, (i.e. are any characteristic beliefs, practices and rituals stable over time?).

So, Millikan's suggestion for how kinds qualify as part of scientific taxonomies is simply too demanding. The templates of higher kinds need not be highly well-focused to guide scientific inquiry about which properties can be projected over their kinds. Once relaxed, the requirements should allow for human *historical* kinds to be higher kinds.

That said, just like many first-order historical kinds might not always be the ones we intuitively pick out (we've seen examples in the case of both species and gender), the higher kinds will not always be the ones we take them to be either. I mentioned the example of Abrahamic religions since the religions that fall under them can plausibly be traced back to a common source. This is unlikely to be true for all kinds that we often consider to be religions. That is because a higher kind follows the same principles as the kinds that fall under it: it only licenses projections and predictions about its instances if there is some common cause among all the kinds that fall under it. For *historical* higher kinds, this means there must be a reproductive chain linking instances to common models. And, I believe it is implausible that *all* religions can be traced back to a common source. So we should identify more plausible candidate higher historical kinds that can be traced back to common sources.

Consider Buddhism as another higher kind. According to Buddhist scholar Cathy Cantwell (2010), there is a commitment among all Buddhist traditions to the three Jewels (the Buddha, the Dharma and the Sangha), the particular initiation rite Going for the Refuge, as well as a few other ethical, ritual and meditative practices. Still, Cantwell claims that probably many more features vary among different Buddhist traditions than are shared among them, with the diversity in Buddhist traditions representing "different historical trajectories of separate lines of descent" (p. 4). So, while there is a common ancestry of the different kinds of Buddhism, many of the central characteristics of the religious practice have changed over time, and some have come to stably vary among different historical branches of the religion.

The general structure then seems to be the following: all branches of Buddhism share a common ancestry, but Buddhism *per se* might not be that inductively fecund because the different traditions have retained in common only a small proportion of the original features. Thus, Buddhism seems more plausible as a higher kind that guides inquiry of the different Buddhist kinds that fall under it. This would parallel the case of the higher kind primates. Some central characteristics are shared by all primates in terms of morphology, anatomy and behavior, but individual primate species (e.g. lemurs, orangutans, hominids) are each bound to have a much richer set of properties for primatologists to study. For the case of Buddhism, this means that we should expect East Asian Buddhism (mostly Mahayana tradition) to be more inductively fecund but less global than Buddhism, but also less fecund and more global than a tradition such as the Soto Zen variety (introduced around the 12th century in China and Japan).

In general, with historical kinds there typically is a trade-off between the *scope* of generalizations on the one hand and the *inductive fecundity* on the other, such that increased scope (i.e. the generalizations govern more instances) comes at the expense of fecundity. As in the case of biological evolution, it is because there is more reproductive fidelity, and hence an increased number of projectable features, the more spatio-temporally proximate the instances are in the cultural evolutionary tree.

Ideally we could also submit the rich data about Buddhism drawn from scholarship and research in anthropology, history and archeology to phylogenetic modeling practices similar to those used in the study of the cultural evolution of tool use and languages. Such modeling and tracing methods might then further help demarcate the relevant lineages (see e.g. Richerson & Boyd, 2005; Lewens, 2015). But it also seems like anthropological and historical research on kinds such as Buddhism already follows such lineage thinking more implicitly (see Cantwell, 2010, for references). As they treat their kinds as explicit *cultural* products, they are often conscious of demarcating the right kinds and wary of generalizing too far across time and space. That is, just as in evolutionary biology, there seems to be an awareness that individuation and study of kinds must respect the temporal and spatial constraints that are tied to the particular origin and distribution of the particular kind under study. The historical kinds account gives a positive spin to these constraints and claims that, despite fluctuation and variation, there is nevertheless a continuity and stability enabled by a chain of reproduction from particular models.

Thus, if we think of kinds of culture in explicit historical terms, it has the capacity to guide our expectations about the scope of our generalizations and how inductively fecund our kind might be. The more temporally distant the reproductive links between ancestors and descendants are, the less likely it is that our inferences from one instance to another will go through and the more likely it is that we should be considering as a higher kind, whose role is to guide inquiry rather than support many generalizations of its own. The closer items are on a lineage, the increased amount of projections we can make across them, but at the expense of a decreased inferential *scope* of these inferences.

So once again, attention and empirical study of the lineages matter for demarcating the right kinds. We should observe the trade-off between inductive scope and richness that comes with the increased distance between items on a lineage. We also need to be open to revising some of our intuitive higher kinds, by for instance replacing putative categories, e.g. *Religion*, with historical (higher) kind categories such as *Abrahamic religions* and *Buddhism*. The latter categories simply give us better templates for the questions to ask of the kinds that fall under them.

## 6.2 The multiple realization of cultural kinds[3]

This brings us to another type of trade-off that I discussed earlier in the book. This one is about the case for *multiple realization* undermining the claim for multiple projectability of the kind (and so, properly speaking, undermining the kindhood itself). Earlier in my critical account of the selected function account of special science kinds (Section 3.1), I argued that the only way to escape such a trade-off is to find a legitimate case of multiply realized kinds where the variation in the physical means of realizing the kinds does not undercut the multiple projectability.

Barring kinds of people (in which I for one fail to make any sense of multiple realization), I think many kinds due to cultural reproduction represent just those cases where there is no trade-off between a kind's multiple projectability and its multiple realization. These cultural kinds do not have characteristic physical features among their determinable properties or questions we might ask of them. Instead, they contain systematically arranged *information or content*, which typically combines factual knowledge about the world and prescriptive or practical know-how that affects human behaviors.

Although the cultural information in question is typically expressed in terms such as "belief systems" or "oral traditions", the truth is that it does not much matter in which physical manner such information is realized. In fact, the social learning responsible for kinds transmission typically exploits the possibility that cultural information is the kind of information that can be expressed by a variety of means such as artefacts, skills, gestures, texts, beliefs and linguistic utterances. And this variation of physical realization occurs without sacrificing precisely the projectable content that interests scientists and others.

Take the kinds of Buddhism again. Here social learning can flexibly employ various means for realizing the projectable cultural content of the religion in different time-slices. We can see it realized in verbal representations, either by the beliefs being referred to in passing or elaborated in discussions and stories; by being embodied in the gestures and behavior of individuals who practice the religion or are converting; and finally, in the religious texts, artefacts, monuments and buildings.

Suppose we have never before encountered a follower of Soto Zen Buddhism and have no familiarity with the religion. If we have had other encounters of other forms of Buddhism, we will have a template of relevant questions to ask (about its origin, characteristic routines and lasting dogmas, say). But among our questions, there will not be any about questions that presuppose a particular physical means to realize the relevant projectable content.

To be clear, here multiple realization is compatible with there being considerable social and psychological conditions and constraints (cognitive and motivational) for social learning to occur – some of which were discussed in the last chapter and others that will be touched on in the next. The key point here is rather that in the case of cultural kinds with different temporal instances as their members, these constraints do not affect the trade-off between, on the one hand, the variation in underlying mechanism for realization and, on the other, the inductive richness. The relevant cultural information clustering together in different time-slices can be reproduced in a variety of flexible and interchangeable ways, none of which constrain the realization of the *product*: i.e. the physical manifestation of the cultural information. The original properties of Buddhism may have been physically realized in an oral tradition, but they can still be reproduced and expressed in the skills, beliefs, artefacts and so on. Thus, neither the social learning mechanisms of observation, imitation and teaching nor its psychological components typically constrain the content in such a way that it needs to be reproduced in the same physical manner as it has been modeled.[4]

Indeed, considering the abundance of physical resources that social learning and human culture has at its disposal for reproducing content, it would be strange if it did *not* use multiple physical means. Consider the information concerning how to attain liberation central to all kinds of Buddhism. It might originally be conveyed by a verbal self-report and then be transmitted in the narratives of the next generation, to then be instantiated in written work and symbols of the religious artefacts – or any other combination of these. In fact, in order to understand, explain and even to apply such knowledge, it makes sense to collect knowledge from various different sources, such as self-reports, narratives, artefacts, texts and so on. Conversely, it does not make much sense to pay attention to the particularities of the physical manifestations of a cultural kind. Increasingly, the cultural content in question is inferred from texts disseminated on the Internet. So, scientists have yet another physical realization of the relevant content – but not one that replaces all others.

The multiple-realization thesis remains compelling for cultural kinds of music, cuisine and different ideologies etc. In fact, both the literature on cultural evolution and more traditional social sciences already operates under the assumption that the content of such kinds might be represented in various physical items such as institutions, artefacts and verbal and non-verbal behavior. I have merely justified their assumption. The beauty of the content of cultural information being socially transmitted is that this is creative: it encourages the reproduction in whichever physical means are available in the culture.

Many kinds that are culturally reproduced can be expressed by a variety of mediums: in artefacts, skills, gestures, music, texts – both offline and online – and in linguistic utterances. This variety is only successfully investigated by also using a variety of different scientific methodologies represented by archaeology, anthropology, literary and linguistic studies, religious studies, musicology and political science. I have also urged that the human sciences have much to learn from biologists' and also mathematicians' work on cultural evolution and their models of cultural stability and change. If anything, this supports the virtue of interdisciplinarity within the human and cultural sciences such that the historical approach to cultural kinds gives us an *ontological rationale* for working beyond disciplinary boundaries. In a slogan, with multiple realization, we also find the need for multiple sciences and their synthesis.

Thus, to conclude, even if multiple realization is not the marker of the human sciences kinds – the individual members of different kinds of people are hardly multiply realized in any meaningful sense, for instance – human kinds are not reducible to physical kinds across the board either. Indeed, many, many cultural kinds are multiply realized, but are typically also neglected by the literature on multiple realization and reduction (probably due to worries about them being "proper" or "real" kinds).

## Notes

1 The example of mercury is taken from Sylvain Bromberger, who makes a similar point to Millikan, but rather than putting it in terms of higher kinds and templates, he puts it in terms of different members of a kind being "models" of each other relative to certain questions (1997, p. 156).

2 This leaves it open as to whether the cognitive ability for such templates is innate or learned.

3 This section draws on material published in Godman (2015).

4 That is not to say that some channels of transmission aren't more important than others for the survival of a cultural kind. Indeed, as a reviewer of this book has put to me, the oral tradition arguably has a very privileged role in comparison to other channels of transmission. Still, very few cultural kinds have needed to survive by oral tradition alone due to the many other opportunities for transmitting content through written work, craft and practice, for example. These days, sadly, many cultures give less of a role for the oral tradition as well.

# 7 How historical kinds achieve a moral standing

> There were tons of refugee families flooding the city, Azerbaijani families fleeing Armenia. They showed up empty handed, without anything. Exactly the same way Armenians fled Baku. And they told the same stories. Oh, it was all identical.
>
> Armenian woman who fled from the 1990 Baku pogrom in Azerbaijan, quoted in *Second-hand time: the last of the Soviets*, by Svetlana Alexievich

In the breakup of the Soviet Union many who were previously united under a common flag and language suddenly turned against their neighbors who had now become a salient other. The Armenian woman quoted above is accounting for her experience fleeing from the 1990 Baku pogrom in Azerbaijan in which the Armenian minority was summoned and either murdered or expelled from the country. Safe in Armenia, she finds that the same kind of pogrom was also occurring there but was now directed toward the Azerbaijanis instead.

What have I got to say about belonging to an ethnic category such as being Armenian or Azerbaijani? In the last three chapters, I have given a template to test whether a putative category refers to a historical kind due to cultural reproduction. First, there must be "models", individuals with a rich cluster of features (in the case of ethnicity, it is likely something such as particular cultural and geographic origins of birth that are signified in their behavior: the adoption of religious, culinary and festive traditions, for example). Second, other individuals in the geographical proximity of these models are either attracted to or, due to pressures in their surroundings, compelled to identify and learn from these models. Third, the pattern of learning is reiterated, and there is as a result, a cultural lineage – in this case of a particular ethnicity.

On the face of it then, individuals who belong to a particular ethnic category seem to belong to historical kinds due to cultural reproduction. Yet this does not explain how an ethnicity can go from being something that individuals hardly reflect upon and that is just a part of their normal daily life to becoming *the* salient part of that individual and a target of highly specific treatment and sanctions. Upon the breakup of the Soviet Union there clearly was a radical transformation of what it meant to be an Armenian or an Azerbaijani. I would urge that if the historical account should truly be an account of human kinds such as ethnicities, this kind of status transformation is something the account should be able to speak to.

Earlier on in this book, we saw that many philosophers of social science and social ontology have taken an interest in the human kinds like race, precisely due to their inhabiting certain status functions at the group level, like the group being the recipient of certain permissions, rights and obligations (Section 3.2). What I found unsatisfactory in the typical explanations of these "curious" properties in Searle's institutional account and Guala's equilibria approach was not the fact that status functions were dependent on some collective attitudes or societal equilibria – they surely are in some sense. Rather, my problem was that these authors' reference to a cumulative change or a collective recognition masks what is really important for most actual social scientific explanations of normative features of groups. Such explanations, I suggested, would involve a reference to the power structure or asymmetry of a particular place and time. Only with this historical specificity, I argued, do we have the explanatory purchase to determine *whose* acceptance, *whose* preferences and *whose* speech acts matter for the emergence of certain statuses.

This cultural and historical specificity seems necessary for explaining many of the normative features of human kinds that we have already discussed. It is a particular patriarchal structure of a certain culture that will determine the permitted labor role of each gender – whether your gender allows you to be a carer or a cardinal, say. It is the religious dominance of Buddhism within a particular society or nation that determines whether a Buddhist believer has the right or even obligation to practice her religion. Race and ethnicity are some of the most poignant examples of status functions conferred by particular communities at a particular time and place (typically, a majority community that sees themselves as belonging to a different race or ethnicity than those that it confers status functions to). There are sadly numerous examples of societies where certain categories of people are singled out for special treatment on the grounds of belonging to a certain "race" or "ethnicity". Such are the quintessential cases of discrimination and apartheid where members of some groups are only permitted to travel within certain parts of a city or forbidden to attend some schools and workplaces. At its most tragic extreme, we find examples like the Baku pogrom.

The elimination of race as a scientific category is thought to be inconsequential from the point of view of politics and policy (e.g. Zack, 2014). However, as I argued in Section 2.4, I think the better argument comes from the other direction. It is precisely *because* we want to resist an oppressive or discriminatory reality that social scientists and philosophers should reveal the reality of belonging to such categories. I have argued that taking groups to be real human kinds where we can track real comparative differences among kinds is one way to begin to uncover potential injustices among groups. But I have yet to show how the *historical* account that purports to disclose a deeper explanatory dimension to this reality can really be of assistance in projects to do with achieving emancipation and a moral standing.[1]

This chapter of the book will therefore develop an account of how historical kinds may undergo status transformations and as a result achieve a moral standing. Some of the general points I will make might also be generalized to related human kinds such as kinds of class[2], sexuality and even gender, where similar status transformations either have occurred or could occur due to certain shifts in political treatment.

It is common to focus on categories of race and ethnicity from the purview of North America, but I want to enrich and diversify the debate by focusing on the categories from a horizon a bit closer to home for me. I will discuss the supposed racial groups in northern Sweden and Finland and a particular status transformation that occurred for the Sámi as part of the racial theorizing at the turn of the 20th century.

## 7.1 Physical anthropology and the Sámi

Racial theorizing in the Nordic region is intimately connected with the eugenics movement that took place in the Nordic countries from the 1930s to as far as the end of the 1970s.[3] Eugenics was often sanctioned by the scientific mainstream, but it also contained a devastating element that were integrated with xenophobic ideologies (Buchanan et al., 2001). Eugenics was, however, preceded by the scientific program of *physical anthropology*, which had less ideological elements but considerable scientific influence in the region. Anders Retzius, the founder, invented an index for measuring craniums toward the end of the 19th century, and physical anthropology had its heyday in the 1920s.

A central assumption of the field was that physical and anatomical features – and particularly the size of the cranium and bodily height (but also facial shape and features, postures and skin tone) – clustered together in commonly recognized kinds of races. The most scrutinized kinds were the Nordic race, the Sámi and the Finns (in addition, Jews; so-called tattare (gypsy) and zigenare (Roma) were also classified distinctly) (Broberg & Roll-Hansen, 2005).

The core hypothesis for investigation was that the cluster of physical features systematically correlated with heritable mental characteristics which were of medical concern. In particular, it was believed that race correlated with presumed heritable conditions of neurosis, epilepsy, alcoholism and mild retardation. The supposed heritability of these conditions in turn led to concerns about their spreading and especially about their "mixing" and being adopted by the "noble" Nordic race.

One of the most documented cases of this research is the Swedish psychiatrist Herman Lundborg who spent extensive time in the Swedish and Finnish north photographing the Sámi and Finns living there as well as documenting their skull measurements (Hagerman, 2015). Craniums were also collected from Sámi gravesites and archived. Lundborg even attempted to find correlations between blood type and race, but without any success. In 1915 Lundborg became the world's first docent and researcher in the subject of racial biology and medical heritability. Six years later, the Swedish parliament decided to grant him a professorship, and the State Institute for Racial Biology was opened in Uppsala in 1922.

The field of physical anthropology and racial biology thus represented less of a popular or populist movement and much more of an authority-driven enterprise, which frequently drew on the professors at German universities as the recognized experts. Herman Lundborg and his counterparts in Finland (Yrjö Karava) and Norway (Alfred Mjöen) all became highly recognized and influential scientists with elected positions in their respective national academies. Yet, despite reaching such stature, they had remarkably little success in actually confirming any of their scientific hypotheses about heritability or about the correlation between supposed racial and psychological traits.

In fact, almost none of the cues that Lundborg, for example, used for his racial classification were physical. They were linguistic, cultural and geographic. In the early 1800s, mother tongue was also thought to be an indicator of biological ancestry and to demarcate a boundary between racial groups in Sweden and Finland (which until 1809 was part of Sweden and until today has an influential Swedish-speaking minority). The focus of Lundborg's research lay in the north of both countries – a region with a long history of multiculturalism, where different mother tongues are still spoken – Swedish, different Sámi languages, Finnish and meänkieli (Finnish with elements of Swedish). While the Finns had been thought of as belonging to a race of Mongol origin, attention to their linguistic roots also prompted a revision where they were thought to belong to an East Baltic race.

The attention to supposed correlations with anatomy and hereditary conditions of researchers of physical anthropology indicates an attempt to move beyond ethnic and cultural differences. One clearly attempted to postulate precisely kinds of races enabled by *biological* reproduction. But filling in the cultural correlations with physical correlations proved difficult for the researchers. Lundborg's work on correlating blood measures with anatomy in the Swedish north was not successful. In Finland alone, 15,000 skull measurements were performed within the population alongside reviews of noses and shapes of the face. Initially the Swedish-speaking authorities of the country tried to support the view that this race was not only distinct, but also inferior compared to the more noble Nordic race. Later on, however, and throughout the 1930s, the research concerning a distinct Finnish race was in fact used to demonstrate a proudly distinct national character of the people in Finland (Hietala, 2005, p. 199f.).

Even setting aside the researcher's massively problematic hierarchical hypotheses about Finns and Sámi in relation to the "Nordic race", there was a dismal failure to establish correlations between physical features and the psychological and medical features of concern (such as epilepsy and retardation). There were also a number of claims of biological *heredity*, especially when it came to the psychological features of groups, that never came close to being substantiated.

It thus seems safe to conclude that the racial *biological* kinds that Lundborg and others supposed existed did not exist.[4] The medical traits that were of interest were not shown to correlate robustly with anatomy, and the heritability claims were for the most part left unsupported. One was able to ascertain some plausibly heritable differences among Swedish- and Finnish-speaking groups in differences in infant mortality at the time (Hietala, 2005), but whether this could be ascribed to biological differences (e.g. incidence of genetic diseases) or to cultural practices (e.g. child-rearing practices) is unclear. I contend that the most robust correlations within the different groups were still found in terms of language and culture, i.e. something which physical anthropologists obscured and neglected rather than built upon. Many of the features that did seem to correlate with one another – livelihood, language, cooking, musical and spiritual practices, for example – were much more likely a result of *cultural inheritance* to common *cultural models*. That is to say that the "race" of the physical anthropologist research programs collapses into what many consider kinds of *ethnicity*.

The mistaken and perhaps ideologically motivated views of the research program of physical anthropology also meant that researchers likely had a number of serious false assumptions about such things as the biological causes of psychological traits, how individuals of a certain race would have distinctive measures of craniums and how they would belong to distinctive blood groups. In the terms employed in this book, the cluster of features thought to mark out racial kinds were not present. Nor were these clusters of properties, or any neighboring clusters, due to biological *common* causes (though some heritable traits may have biological causes). At the same time, there is a plausible case for there being ethnic groups with a partially different cluster of properties due to cultural inheritance and social learning from common cultural models.

## 7.2 The status transformation of the Sámi

Considering what groups have the potential to be real historical kinds in this history is liable to miss the moral of the tale. In particular, it would overlook the effect that the powerful authorities at the time, especially those of *scientific* authority, have on the (ethnic) kinds in question. I might have persuaded you that a shared reproduction to common models might explain why properties *come together* in different instances, but if we are in pursuit of an explanation of their considerable transformation as a result of their interactions with researchers, it will not help much to say that what these researchers thought of as race was false or that it was, in fact, ethnicity.

The status transformation at the time for the Sámi was tied not only to the racial studies of physical anthropologists, but also to other events at the time. Important examples include the forcible relocation of individuals across the newly minted national borders from Norway into Sweden and also the forced Christian schooling of children (Labba, 2020). Indeed, it has been suggested that the field studies of Lundborg and others were part of a colonial attempt to justify the appropriation of the wealth of natural resources found in the region (Hagerman, 2017). These and other experiences with authorities may have led to status transformations in their own right. (They are also often shared among many indigenous groups around the world, and therefore mark a natural place to start if one wants to generalize the arguments I want to make in the following two sections.) I will, however, focus on the contribution and effects of racial research done by physical anthropologists.

The central part of the status transformation for Sámi at the time seems to be the felt experience of being of, or belonging to, an inferior race. While there is hardly any psychological study of this phenomenon (which scientific authority would have cared at this time?), it is noted anecdotally from those who experienced the process and in the accounts of descendants (see e.g. Hagerman, 2015; Labba, 2020). Supposing there was such an experience, what brought it about? There is some debate about the extent to which this scientific practice of physical anthropologists was motivated by ideology and overt or covert racism, according to which some races were seen as inherently inferior and degenerate compared with others (see Hagerman, 2017 *vs*. Wasniowski, 2017a, 2017b). Still, it is agreed that the research into race in the Nordics was broadly aimed at targeting a perceived qualitative decrease in the mental capacities of the national population that was thought to occur via racial mixing. There was also a natural counterpart to this research in the new welfare states of the Nordic countries adopting several policies of *positive* eugenics (e.g. monetary rewards) for encouraging the reproduction of the "healthy members of the Nordic race" (Broberg & Roll-Hansen, 2005).

Thus, researchers who conducted the field studies need not even have been explicitly or implicitly racist to hold some beliefs about their own relative superiority in comparison to the subjects of their study. The research methods and practice itself *embodied* the idea of a comparative superiority of researchers in relation to the subjects of the research. The views of inferiority were ongoingly expressed through the photography sessions, the cranium measurements and, indeed, the whole practice of singling out individual Sámi and Finns in the region for study expressed the view that only members of these groups had the "inferior traits". Moreover, implicit in this research was the idea that the epistemic *authority* was in the hands of the researcher vis-á-vis their scientific subjects.

I contend that the significant status transformation was therefore caused by the humiliation and feeling of inferiority that resulted from these physical anthropologist studies with the result that many Sámi members, in particular, but also to some extent Finns, experienced a new sense of inferiority and indignation.

Another example of traits that are adopted to fit with the representations of those in power might be Lundborg's and other's assumptions about the *homogeneity* among the Sámi and their herding livelihood. In actual fact, it is likely that this idea of homogeneity within the group did not actually capture the actual cultural lineages. What was grouped together as a single race of Sámi was at the time more likely at least four ethnic groups of the northern part of the Scandinavian peninsula (including not only Sweden, Finland and Norway but also Russia): the Fell Sámi, Forest Sámi, Coast Sámi and the Skolt Sámi or Skolts, all with distinct languages and practices of livelihood (there were probably several more groups if one is to truly respect the geographic, linguistic and cultural constraints on reproduction that existed at the time). Over time, however, it seems these expectations of the scientists may have contributed to assimilation and convergence in the streams of inheritance among different groups, thereby generating some of the looping effects described by Hacking (Section 3.3.2).[5]

For these psychological beliefs of homogeneity or feelings of inferiority to be lasting within the group, two more conditions would have had to be present: first, the relevant trait(s) must be *robustly adopted* among different Sámi members of the group at the time and, second, the trait(s) must be *heritable*. For simplicity I'll focus on the traits of perceived inferiority from now on.

How would these traits be adopted within the group exactly? Those working on cultural evolution who standardly ask this kind of question tend to rely on notions of either individual or group "fitness" as an account of a trait's adoption. For fitness there must be some reproductive advantage to the individual or advantage to the group's survival (Richerson & Boyd, 2005). But why suppose that it is a matter of individual fitness? As Richard Lewontin and Joseph Fracchia have argued, this ignores the possibility that it is "power that can force a trait's 'selection'" (Fracchia & Lewontin, 2005, p. 22).[6] That is, powerful groups and individuals can determine the retention of biological and cultural traits (Lewens, 2015).

This might seem familiar from an earlier discussion. Recall that Ron Mallon (2016), in his account of human kinds, emphasized how out-group representations can change the behavior of those who belong to a minority category directly (Section 3.3.3). He argued that it is strategic, or at least rational, for, say, members of an ethnic minority to modify their actions in accordance with those representations. This seems especially plausible in the case where those responsible for the out-group representation are of such an authority that they can determine the reward structure of conforming to a behavior. The trait of a sense or feeling of inferiority fits well with the expectations of researchers, and such a trait might simply have adopted to accord with the expectations of those with power.

More importantly, though, for a status transformation of a group to last or be *sustained*, some characteristics of the representations must not only be robustly adopted, they must eventually also be passed on to others. There are two possible vehicles for this: non-genetic biological inheritance, often called *epigenetic* inheritance, and social learning. Let's begin with the former.

Non-genetic inheritance of acquired characteristics should not sound as crazy these days as it did at one time when it was thought that no *acquired* characteristics could be inherited. It remains true that acquired characteristics cannot be inherited through rewriting our genes, but we have already seen many examples of non-genetic inheritance in this book, such as cultural learning. There is also a growing field of epigenetic inheritance that looks at means of inheriting acquired traits in non-human animals such as mating songs in killer whales, habitat imprinting mechanisms in insects and sexual preferences in birds (Jablonka & Raz, 2009; for a broad rationale of non-genetic inheritance, see Mameli, 2004).

In fact, there are some indications that fearful and traumatic experiences are precisely the kind of traits that can be transmitted epigenetically from parents to offspring. In one experiment on laboratory mice, the mice were trained to fear the smell of acetophenone, a chemical the scent of which has been compared to those of cherries and almonds. The mice were trained to fear this smell by being given small electric shocks when exposed to the smell. After learning to associate the scent with pain (evidenced by shuddering in the presence of acetophenone even without a shock), their fearful reaction to the smell was also passed on to their pups. The inherited reaction could even be demonstrated in a third generation of mice – the "grandchildren" (Dias & Ressler, 2014).

The researchers propose that DNA methylation, which modifies the expression of genes, is responsible for this effect, but the precise mechanisms for these epigenetic effects are under debate. There is also evidence of how the lasting stress and anxiety of trauma in humans, for example Holocaust survivors, can lead to their offspring having a similar type of methylation changes, which suggests that the psychological effects of trauma are also epigenetically heritable in humans (Yehuda et al., 2016). So, the feelings of inferiority and indignation in response to traumatic encounters with (multiple) authorities might very well be ones that parents tend to transmit intergenerationally within their ethnic group.

These effects can however also be transmitted via social learning and, if so, not merely between parents and offspring, but also between other adults and children (by the former being role models, say). The inheritance and learning of such "maladaptive" traits have been considered a puzzle in the cultural evolution literature; why would we learn the behavior of models, even if it is detrimental *overall* to oneself and even to one's group? Why would traits like indignation or inferiority still be passed on?

In my view the answers available in the cultural evolution literature about why we socially transmit maladaptive traits, too, are quite flawed. Peter Richerson and Robert Boyd, for example, hypothesize cognitive biases such as *conformist biases* – the tendency to copy the most common variant of local practice – and *content biases* – the tendency to copy variants that are easy to remember and transmit – to explain the reliable retention and inheritance of socially learned traits (2005). But it is unclear how much this accommodates traits that do not (yet) represent the most prevalent or the most memorable strategies.

Another proposal to this puzzle harks back to Hacking's idea of a moral cultural niche (Section 3.3.2). Kim Sterelny has developed the notion of cultural niche construction, which locates the bias for social learning in the environment, rather than in our cognition (2006). Though Sterelny focuses on quite different types of cultural traits such as tool use, cooperative norms and agriculture, it is not hard to see how it might apply to a case such as ethnicity. The idea is simply that our environments contain cultural-specific information (such as narratives, scripts and artefacts) that scaffold the learning and thus, in the case of ethnicity, whatever information is relevant to one's group belonging. One instance of this would be the labeling effects and introduction of pictures of people termed Sámi or "Lapps" (as the supposed group was somewhat derogatorily referred to at the time) that influence and constrain the social learning and contribute to the transformation of what it means to belong to kind (Hacking, 2007a). Certainly, the historical-reproductive account can embrace the bias that comes with being born and brought up within a particular cultural niche where there simply are not many alternative models available. But when the trait seems particularly disadvantageous, we might not be convinced that the reference to a cultural niche is sufficient.

My sense is that *social motivational biases* must be added in addition to the cognitive and environmental scaffolding to explain how a maladaptive trait like feeling shameful and inferior can be heritable. In previous work, I have argued that for humans as a species, the motivation that is the most dominant for our learning about ourselves and our surroundings is simply the inherent value of sociality; or, simply, social motivations (Godman, 2013; Godman, Nagatsu, & Salmela, 2014).[7] The role of social motivations in learning is to privilege or bias such information that can be attained from imitation, mimicry and also observations of the action of others through allowing for a closer affiliation and sense of belonging with others. So, children might learn to feel shameful and inferior, particularly in their interaction with authorities and the majority society – not because parents and elders want their children to inherit these traits, but because this is a learned means of conforming and affiliating with one's group.

The importance of these social motivations to belong finds their support in developmental and comparative psychology, where they are strong contenders for explaining the human-specific propensity for so-called *overimitation*. Chimpanzees typically can copy full behavioral sequences involved in a task design but tend to eliminate redundant components of the sequence when the causal relation between actions and outcomes become apparent. Humans, on the other hand, overimitate – that is, we do not reach the goal in the most effective way possible but instead try to do it in precisely the way it has been modeled to us (Horner & Whiten, 2005). Subsequent studies have shown that children begin to overimitate at the age of two and have an increased tendency to overimitate, and that adults do it just as much as five-year-olds do (McGuigan, Makinson, & Whiten, 2011). Finally, children overimitate at a high frequency in all communities worldwide (Nielsen & Tomaselli, 2010).

In my view, the social motivations to belong provide a compelling explanation of the human prevalence of overimitation (see also Nielsen & Blank,

2011). The thought is simply that reproducing the complete modeled actions of another human being is more important for us than merely producing the outcomes more efficiently. These results cannot be attributed to failures of *competence*, as that very competence seems to be demonstrated in chimpanzees, according to the Horner and Whiten test. So, imitation, overimitation and social learning more generally is not merely about competence and a means of learning skills; these behaviors also function as means of engaging with others, which in turn facilitates the formation of relationships and social bonds (Užgiris, 1981).

From an evolutionary perspective, the importance of social motivations in guiding our learning is hardly surprising. There are probably many species that can rightly be described as "social", but it is often thought that only humans qualify as the "hyper-social species" (Richerson & Boyd, 2005). In particular, the pan-cultural human ability to form social bonds both with kin and non-kin is recognized as important from the viewpoint of biological and cultural evolution alike (Chevallier, Kohls, Troiani, Brodkin, & Schultz, 2012).

But social motivations are not unequivocally a good thing for us. While social motivations can lead us to behave in ways so that we fit in and learn useful traits, they can also be individually maladaptive, such as in the case of experiencing inferiority and indignation as a result of seeing your parents display associated expressions and behavior. It can also be learnt by witnessing (other) role models' behavior interactions with authorities.[8] I thus conclude that social motivations involved in learning from models are key components for explaining how disadvantageous traits like feelings of inferiority and denigration can get passed on in culture.

***

Let's take stock. In the last section I have argued that the purported kinds of race used in Nordic physical anthropology did not in fact exist. Instead, there are good reasons to consider that there were some real historical kinds of ethnicity, i.e. kinds principally due to the existence of cultural niches and social learning of language and other traits. But my focus in this section has been to show how the studies of physical anthropologists led to lasting changes to what it meant to belong to the group of Sámi (and to a certain extent also Finns of the region). To exemplify this transformation, I have discussed some different psychological traits, such as a sense of indignation and inferiority among the Sámi population, which have plausibly originated in encounters with the so-called authorities of racial hygiene research (and also in interactions with "authorities" in other related colonial or oppressive practices). I have then shown how in principle both biological and cultural pathways would allow for this inheritance.

The transformations I have considered so far seem almost exclusively negative – both for the individual and for the group to which they belong – but the group might achieve a certain moral standing precisely in recognition of the injustices. Take the case when a government recognizes that a historical injustice has been perpetrated against the Sámi and grants current members special minority or indigenous rights. While many believe that this practice of granting groups rights in response to a past injustice is justified, it remains contested as it is understood as an injustice of the past, perpetrated against past members, but where only present members receive the benefits. This brings me to venture into some truly normative questions, such as can the historical account of human kinds be drawn on to explain why certain groups achieve a moral standing and even support the case of certain group rights?

## 7.3 Historical kinds and emergent group rights

National governments are often slow in implementing the appropriate legislation when it comes to indigenous rights. Only in August 2019 were 25 Sámi craniums repatriated to their original gravesite in Lykselse, Sweden, after being removed for research purposes and later stored away in a museum. In the same year a landmark decision was also made by the Swedish Supreme Court to grant special fishing and hunting rights to Girjas "sameby" (sameby is a legally recognized collective of individual Sámi).

The idea that *current* members of Sámi should be granted group rights *in virtue of* their ethnic membership remains contested, however (see e.g. Pogge, 1997). Such claims about group rights and compensation seem to suppose that the Sámi membership is what allows one to be the recipient of special rights and protections compared to the rest of society, even supposing there is no evidence that current individuals are discriminated against or in other ways treated unjustly. So, can we go beyond explaining how a group goes through a status transformation to arrive at a *normative explanation* of why this *should* also lead to a change in moral standing of the group?

Notice that granting group rights based on an individual's supposed special moral standing need not be with reference to historical events, such as we saw in the last section. What is necessary is that the individual rightholder is entitled to rights *qua* being a member of a group with a certain moral standing.[9] Rights based on the likelihood of facing *current injustices –* often referred to as *structural injustices –* have the same form. Affirmative action and other proactive anti-discrimination policies toward women might, for instance, be justified on the grounds that women as a group are *currently likely* to face structural injustice *or* with reference to historical injustices (or both).[10] As another example, some countries grant asylum in virtue of membership in discriminated or persecuted groups of ethnicity or sexuality without individuals thereby having to show that they have been persecuted or discriminated against. In fact, even the likelihood that an *individual* is likely to face discrimination or some other injustice is a likelihood that she faces *qua* being a member of a particular group.

Political philosophy and political theory are typically concerned with different issues than the principles for individuating and deciding membership, such as deciding the principles for the distribution of goods within already given populations. At the same time, this question arguably lingers in the background. As Michael Walzer points out in his seminal *Spheres of Justice*: "We assume an established group and a fixed population and so we miss the first and most important distributive question: how is that group constituted?" (1983, p. 31). Equally, the highly influential Iris Marion Young worries about the feminist movement abandoning both essentialism and any other criteria for membership: "The naming of women as a specific and distinct collective, moreover is a difficult achievement and one that gives feminism its specificity as a political movement" (1994, p. 718).

I think the notion of membership implicit in the account of historical kinds can be of much help to many discussions, but I will focus on the case for group rights based on the racial studies of the Sámi in the Nordic north discussed in the last sections. I will attempt to make some initial arguments to the conclusion that membership in a historical kind such as the Sámi does grant a special moral standing for individuals of the group such that they might rightly deserve the group rights such as the land, livelihood and language rights that come up for discussion. The hope is that some principles that I will employ in my arguments might generalize as a result of analogous considerations for moral standing among other human historical kinds. But, as with the other cases of this book, we need to approach the purported generalizability with caution. In fact, my intent here is not a finished proposition of principles for group rights but rather to introduce a plausible and intriguing proposal about how the normative features of membership can be approached from a historical kind horizon.

The first benefit to an approach to membership in terms of historical kinds is its potential to unify some existing suggestions. When political philosophers and theorists do venture into the discussion of the potential basis for membership, they typically have a specific type of group in mind. In the debates concerning immigration and the rights of *resident migrants*, Josef Carens has proposed a prioritization of *social membership with temporal and regional proximity* (Carens, 2013 cf. Lim, 2014). In Will Kymlicka's celebrated defense of minority rights (1998), the presence of *historical* (or, perhaps, hypothetical) *agreement* justifies membership-specific rights. In discussions of nationhood, we have influential criteria such as "communitarian embeddedness and reciprocity" (Walzer, 1983) or "mutual belief extended in history" (Miller, 1993). And in feminist political philosophy, we have Young's proposal of thinking of gender as a "serial collective" – a linkage that roughly results from a certain set of historical conditions (1994).

One response to these different and potentially conflicting criteria for deciding group membership is to adopt some form of membership pluralism (e.g. Risse, 2016). I have already mentioned a similar pluralist move in philosophy of science, which rejects any shared and deeper criteria of membership and favors classification according to different scientific interests and domains of inquiry (see e.g. Dupré, 1995; Magnus, 2012). For political discussions, this would then roughly mean deciding membership based on the relevant group or group right in question. Sociologist Roger Brubaker has endorsed eliminativism of the categories of ethnicity and nationality on related grounds (2004). Another form of pluralism or eliminativism regarding membership concerns the priority of our shared cosmopolitan identity (Appiah, 2005). I, however, doubt these strategies remove the need to define membership since even pluralism still has to decide what counts as a legitimate interest (domain, discipline- or purpose-specific) and criteria for membership (or, for eliminativists, why a certain category should be eliminated and not others).

This pushes us back to the very same debates about membership and kind individuation that I have been having in this book. I have argued throughout this book that epistemic reasons imply that all group memberships are not equal (*White horses* are not equal to *Horses* and cross-cultural gender categories are not equal to those defined by a lineage). The same goes for moral reasons. Some groups seem to deserve a moral standing and others do not. This compels us to prioritize some categories over others but also explain why this is so.

As an alternative to pluralism, I then propose there is a central principle capable of unifying the different criteria of membership given by political philosophers and theorists. First, that membership must exhibit a historical continuity such as the one provided by the historical reproductive account I have offered in this book. That is, whether an account ties social membership to the proximate community, the social embeddedness and reciprocity, the extended mutual belief or a historical agreement, there must be some *objective historical relation* or continuity among members. In other words, a historical continuity or relation among members must first be in place in order to be able to pick out which group of individuals the "mutual belief" or "embeddedness" is supposed to apply to. For example, if the living members of a particular group should be compensated for historical injustices such as slavery and colonialism that were only faced by non-living members, there at least has to be some objective historical continuity between the individuals of the past and the individuals of the present for such claims to get off the ground in the first place.

This would be analogous to how individual rights (and responsibilities) rely on some continuity of personal identity over time. If Cecilia was not the same person as when she passed the driver's test, she would not be entitled to drive with a driver's license in her name. If Jenny was not the same person who sent the hateful letter to me, I would not be right to blame her for it. The different time-slices of Cecilia and Jenny must be connected to one another for claims about rights and responsibilities to get off the ground.[11] Similarly, then, for groups with claims for rights (and perhaps also responsibilities – but let us set aside the discussion of responsibilities, as it is another kettle of fish), a minimal condition for attributing rights is that there is an objective connection between the individuals of a group at different points of time and space.

If individuals are connected with one another through a process of cultural reproduction to a common model such as I have argued is the case for certain kinds of gender and ethnicity, this clearly demonstrates historical continuity between them. So, membership in a historical kind provides a natural way to substantiate the necessary historical relation that underpins the rights of a group. Put differently, if there is no such connection via biological or cultural reproduction, we would need some other argument to be convinced that individuals, distributed over time and space, are really members of the same group.

But, as in the case of a single individual, the historical continuity, although necessary for membership rights, is not going to be sufficient. Some historical kinds display continuity but are clearly not deserving of moral standing. Take the putative cultural historical category, *White supremacists*, where certain beliefs, practices and norms are socially learned and could plausibly be passed on from some original models. The series of individuals belonging to this chain fulfill the first condition of historical continuity (and arguably some other conditions in the existing literature, such as embeddedness), but clearly such members should not be candidates for group rights in virtue of their membership (determined by their historical continuity) alone. If we are to make any further progress on the basis of a moral standing and group rights, we need some additional *normative* argument in addition to the historical continuity.

In fact, I think the account of historical reproductive kinds that I have presented in connection to ethnicity and gender allows us to be more ambitious with respect to explaining the moral standing. If we look at the effects of the status transformation of a group, such as the ones discussed in the last sections, three normative arguments for groups rights suggest themselves:

1    The *inheritance* of unjustly acquired traits within a historical kind;
2    The *repeatable* subordination targeting a lineage;
3    The *resultant solidarity* that arises in response to 1 and 2.

Let's begin with (1). In the last section, I argued that the reproductive lineage of the Sámi will after the unjust interference of certain scientific, political and religious authorities such as the different physical anthropology studies, bring about the adoption and transmission of the detrimental psychological traits. For simplicity, I will stick to the example where both Sámi adults and children had to pose for photographs and were recruited for anatomical measurements. I argued that this kind of denigrating and humiliating treatment led to the acquisition of what I will call, "psychological scars" such as a sense of inferiority, shame and indignation. I further argued that such psychological scars were likely transmitted – epigenetically or through social learning – alongside the other practices and characteristics that were modeled in the behavior of the ethnic group.

This transmission of unjustly acquired features would then allow current members to make claims about reparations and compensation for past events not only on behalf of their ancestors but also on behalf of *themselves*. Thus, we have rights that seem to correctly apply on the level of the group as a whole – or at least since the time of the unjustly acquired features. Of course, not all individuals belonging to an ethnic group inherit all the traits of their ancestors. Still, the fact that we can trace such psychological scars of past injustice by tracing the biological and cultural inheritance of traits in many contemporary individual members is a real possibility that should be addressed in the literature on group rights.

In the case of gender, both arguments (1) and (2) seem plausible: either the unjust practice has chiefly occurred in the past and given rise to culturally heritable psychological scars such as a similar sense of inferiority and lack of confidence among members (notice, however, that the biological transmission is much less plausible in this case, since biological parent-offspring transmission is not involved in the transmission of gender traits). But it is also possible that practices of *subordination* ongoingly targeting individual members of the group such that it is highly likely that an individual currently has been exposed *qua* being a member of a group. Suppose that this subordination occurs continually in the more historically sensitive way of categorizing gender that I argued for in Chapter 5. I take it that the latter scenario is typically what people mean by a *structural injustice* when members face an *ongoing* subordination along economic, social, political and legal dimensions in a cultural system. This is also the subordination that Haslanger takes as central to defining what a woman is (2000).

The acts of subordination or demeaning treatment of certain groups or historical kinds therefore warrant a case for a moral standing of the group, both if the unjust events are more distal or more proximal. What is important for the normative arguments in my view are then some *empirical issues*. For argument (1), it is about the likelihood of psychological scars being *adopted* and then *transmitted* either biologically or culturally to new members. For argument (2), what should be evaluated is whether current individuals *qua* members are likely to face the ongoing subordination (so here again the point about being able to demarcate an individual *qua* member is key for the claim about moral standing and group rights). These two arguments are independent, but they are not mutually exclusive, and so they might bolster each other when we ask whether a group merits a particular right to land, language or monetary compensation, for example.

The third possible argument I want to mention does not seem independent of the other two, but rather conditional upon at least one of them being true. It says that precisely *because* of the unjustly acquired and heritable psychological scars or the repeated subordination facing different members of one's group, a *solidarity* with other members might emerge as part and parcel of the cultural reproduction. Certainly, it is often observed that a common plight among members tends to increase their sense of affiliation and solidarity within a lineage. This sense of belonging is often needed for mobilization and joint action, which in turn is arguably needed for the campaign for minority and group rights in the first place. It follows that the special solidarity might merit protection in its own right in the cases of historical and structural injustices, but probably not in cases of solidarity within and outside lineages where it is not in response to any objective subordination or injustice.

Values of solidarity and affiliation are admittedly ones that should not be restricted to members within single lineages, but ones we would wish to apply more broadly. Indeed, in the case of both gender and ethnicity, I mentioned situations where solidarity might spread *across* lineages through witnessing individuals facing analogous treatment. In the case of the Sámi, for example, there has been a takeover of homes and livelihood (particularly the decline in reindeer herding during the 19th and 20th centuries) due to new borders, mining, forestry and, more recently, climate change. The fact that many other indigenous groups have faced these plights and are facing them around the world has likely fostered much common solidarity and common advocacy among indigenous groups more generally.

Still, my sense is that this care and solidarity might nevertheless first need to develop in terms of more local membership, for successful mobilization as well as for spreading more universally. Thus, it seems that the care and solidarity might first require protection precisely in local terms. This would give us some additional support for offering rights according to religion, ethnicity, gender and sexuality. I admit this third argument is more objectionable than the others. It certainly has to be weighed against the problems of defending too far-reaching identity politics where the care about one's particular group and its members might start to trump either individual rights or the obligations of citizens.

You may also have noticed that the argument from solidarity draws on features that are closely related to what others have advocated in political philosophy and theory, such as community, reciprocity and embeddedness.[12] In contrast to them, though, I believe the argument for solidarity is not only defeasible, but only to be taken seriously if the other two considerations are in play – i.e. a repeatable subordination and a transmission of unjustly acquired traits. In other words, while certain white supremacist groups may certainly also exhibit solidarity, community, reciprocity as well as historical continuity, this does not mean they deserve any group rights.

## 7.4 Summary

In this chapter I have made several arguments. I have shown how some supposedly racial kinds of past human sciences such as physical anthropology were much more likely ethnic kinds enabled primarily by the cultural transmission of traits. More importantly, however, I hope to have shown how an account of historical kinds can explain how certain status transformations can have lasting impacts for descendant members with the biological or cultural transmission of psychological scars. One example is the one we began with: the Baku pogrom and the resulting effects for both Azerbaijanis and Armenians. Another is the racial hygiene research of physical anthropologists in the Nordic north at the beginning of the 20th century and its lasting effects for the Sámi and Finns of the region.

The good news, I believe, is that states and societies might – and, I have argued, *should* – also introduce rights and a moral standing for these groups in recognition of such unjust events and their effects. This last section has explored three novel normative arguments for such group rights suggested by the historical kind account. I surmise that analogous arguments might be applied to other indigenous groups around the world as well as genders, ethnicities, sexualities and maybe even social classes that face analogous historical or structural injustices.

## Notes

1 Thanks to Anneli Jefferson for suggesting this term to me.
2 For reasons of space, this book unfortunately does not discuss the rich category of social class. I would like to make a small suggestion, however, and that is that although instinctively social class is an economic category and not a historical kind, I believe class models can also become a prominent model for social learning. But what kind of categorization scheme we should adopt for class is probably a very complicated matter, and clearly merits its own discussion. For some interesting gestures about the scientific category of class, see Kincaid (2016).

3 It is estimated that 63,000 Swedes, mostly women, were sterilized in the period between 1935–1975 in accordance with certain sterilization laws. Similar laws were in effect in Finland, Denmark and Norway. For the latter decades, however, race was much less of a determinant for sterilization compared to an alleged mental disability or disorder (Hietala, 2005).

4 This leaves open that a more modern cladistic concept of race could somehow be applicable to the people of this region. But these cladistic kinds are unlikely to map on to the categories and clusters used in the physical anthropologist's study (e.g. Andreasen, 2005).

5 On a positive side, the mistaken expectations may inadvertently have led to an increased solidarity among members of different Sámi groups (but there are also indications of an increased rivalry between groups in response to these expectations). As with many indigenous groups, there has also been considerable pressure toward assimilation with the majority culture (Valkonen, Valkonen, & Koivurova, 2016).

6 I might not be so guilty of this particular charge since I have quite explicitly argued that an account of historical kinds in cultural evolution does best to depart from adaptationist and teleological commitments.

7 Following Cecilia Heyes, we can think of these motivations as input mechanisms for our learning process, where they have the role of privileging information from social channels over others, e.g. information provided by people in our environment (2012). That is why social learning need not only represent information provided by imitation or mimicry, but also pure observation of social stimuli (without interacting with it).

8 Social rewards are not the only source of rewards (and withdrawn reward or sanctions are not the only form of punishments) that bias social learning. The existing cultural niche is another, as are purely material rewards (in the case of the Sámi, some monetary rewards and punishments were connected to the threat of land loss, for example). Indeed, it might be tricky to model the effects of different rewards separately (Godman et al., 2014).

9 A different kind of group rights often shows up in the social ontology literature, namely, the rights of organized collectives such as boards, governments and non-governmental organizations (NGOs) (Epstein, 2018). If such collectives have rights (and responsibilities) at all, I am sure it will demand a different kind of defense from the one offered here, so they are not my concern.

10 The justification of affirmative action comes in various different forms; structural and historical injustice are but two different forms. For an important discussion, see Lippert-Rasmussen (2020).

11 Thanks to Helen Beebee for first making this salient to me.

12 It may also be worth noting how this type of defense of minority rights is separated from Will Kymlicka's (1998) contractualism that appeals to an actual historical or hypothetical *agreement* between parties. Indeed, these arguments might offer independent support.

# 8    Conclusion

## The key contributions of human historical kinds

So, we are at the end, and I have not been able to discuss many other human kinds in this relatively short book. I have mentioned sexuality, class and cultural (psychiatric) syndromes a few times in passing as I believe there are indications of how reproductive chains to models may be responsible for property correlations in these cases as well. Still what should we say about other candidate kinds supporting a range of comparative tendencies of which there are surely many more in the human sciences?

My own case study approach should demonstrate why diverse kinds in the human sciences are unlikely to all fit neatly into a singular mold. It may for instance be that we need to rethink both some of our intuitive human categories and principles for categorization before we arrive at the right historical kinds in the relevant domain. It might also be that the historical kind account is just not as comprehensive as social constructivist, bare projectability or simple causal accounts of (human) kinds. But keep in mind that comprehensiveness of the account was never the important aim or virtue. I have argued that the important kinds – the real kinds, if you will – permit many, many generalizations, and that this must result from common causes shared by members. There are many categories that will fail to be such kinds. I also argued that the accounts that aim for full comprehensiveness tend to leave important philosophical and moral questions to one side; most notably, what is responsible for the kind's projectability, which is not bare but multiple, and how can certain human categories achieve a moral standing?

I have argued that an account of historical kinds based on the cultural reproduction among its members can answer these questions. There are also answers to common-cause questions that appeal to proximate intrinsic mechanisms, but these remain unpromising in the case of human kinds. For reasons mentioned in Chapter 3 and 5, I doubt functional common causes will work as well. Maybe there are other types of common causes in the case of human kinds. I am genuinely curious to find out, so please get in touch with me if you have some plausible candidate.

In any case, I hope to have convinced you that what the historical kind account possibly loses in comprehensiveness, it makes up for in terms of informativeness and usefulness both for the science that studies these kinds and the policymakers that make decisions based on them. Here are the main claims that I have argued for in this book:

1   Kinds supporting multiple empirical generalizations can come about through a chain of copying or reproduction to a common model. These kinds are *historical kinds*. Reproduction from models – an organism, a type of person, a system of belief – is a powerful mechanism for producing new instances with rich correlations of properties (see Chapters 4, 5 and 6).

2   For human beings, *culture* has proved to be hugely important for the creation of human kinds, such as gender, ethnicity and religion. Culture provides us both with the *means* of reproducing traits and the *models* available (see Chapters 5 and 7). Finally, both social motivations to belong and pressures to conform explain why cultural models take a hold on us. The historical kind framework should be adopted without any adaptationist or teleological commitments (Section 5.3).

3   The lineages of historical kinds suggest an improved way of individuating and demarcating kinds for induction. Particular lineages can better demarcate by, for example:

   a   Encouraging reclassifications. The framework does not leave all our categories as they are and gives principled reasons for a system of (re)classification according to lineages to common models. This can bring about changes to how we understand both the extension of our categories (e.g. *Women*, Chapter 5) and the scope of our inductive generalizations (e.g. *Buddhism*, Chapter 6).

   b   Recognizing a trade-off between the scope of how many instances one's generalizations applies to and how many generalizations one can perform based on a historical kind. Basically, over longer periods of time, an increased number of instances are covered by generalizations but a decreased amount of generalizations can be made (Section 6.1).

   c   Replacing putative *higher categories* that are not based on common causes (e.g. *Religion*) with categories (or higher kinds) that are (e.g. *Abrahamic religions* and *Buddhism*) so as to have a better grasp of what questions are relevant to pose about the (potentially newly discovered) kinds that fall under them (Section 6.1).

4   Multiple realization is alive and well in culture, which can use a variety of physical means to produce new instances of the same kinds (e.g.

beliefs, artefacts, practices, written works). Whereas there is a trade-off between the inductive richness and the variable realization of functionally defined kinds (Section 3.1), it does not exist for cultural kinds (Section 6.2).

5    Human historical kinds are highly malleable in response to power dynamics of the surrounding society and therefore also susceptible to *status transformations*. A morally significant status transformation occurs when some majority or authorities with power lead members of a historical kind of people to adopt traits that are subsequently transmitted on to the lineage. Transmission can occur either via biological epigenetic reproduction or via social learning (Sections 7.1 and 7.2).

6    Historical kinds can achieve a moral standing and support group rights as a result of these status transformations. I offered three related normative arguments for this via the inheritance of unjustly acquired psychological scars among members, the repeatability of subordination to members within a lineage and, finally, the resulting solidarity within a lineage (Section 7.3).

Certainly, membership in historical kinds is not like what has been claimed for some natural kinds, i.e. intrinsic to the individual, inevitable or unchangeable. But that does not mean it is socially constructed either.[1] It is determined by the culturally available models of different kinds of people and the processes by which we learn from others. Historical kinds are also not socially constructed in the sense that belonging to a category is not wholly, or even mostly, about someone's perception or representation – although there are certainly also powerful societal pressures to comply with others' expectations. Fundamentally, I have suggested that kinds of people connected via cultural reproduction come about by individual agents' own need to affiliate with and learn from others.

I have also detected a different way in which the existing power asymmetries in a society can impact human kinds, which importance I believe has not been detected by constructivists. Many human kinds can achieve a moral standing as a result of the psychological scars being transmitted in a lineage. This means that even current members rightly *deserve* to be the recipients of certain rights based on past injustices. It is unclear whether social constructivists can really make any arguments about group rights, as they tend to deny that there is an objective way of demarcating human kinds.

Of course I share the aim of many social constructivists to have societies without both unremedied historical injustices and a subordination of certain groups. But I believe as long as we do have these problems, we will have to set our hopes with the sciences for detecting injustices among groups and the justice and recognition that granting group rights gives.

## Note

1 Of course, social constructivism of human kinds is also a big family of accounts, including Sally Haslanger's (briefly described in Section 2.4), John Searle's (Section 3.2) and Ron Mallon's (Section 3.3.3) and most recently Ásta's (2018). These accounts are different from one another, but I take it that my account contrasts with them all in the ways mentioned.

# Bibliography

Alexandrova, A. (2018). Can the science of well-being be objective? *The British Journal for the Philosophy of Science, 69*(2), 421–445.

Alexievich, S. (2013). *Secondhand time: The last of the Soviets*, trans. Bela Shayevich. Random House Trade.

Andreasen, R. O. (2005). The meaning of "race": Folk conceptions and the new biology of race. *The Journal of Philosophy, 102*(2), 94–106.

Anscombe, G. E. M. (1957). *Intention*. Cambridge, MA: Harvard University Press.

Appiah, K. A. (2005). *The ethics of identity*. Princeton, NJ: Princeton University Press.

Armstrong, D. M. (1980). *Nominalism & realism: Universals & scientific realism* (Vol. 1). Cambridge: Cambridge University Press.

Ásta. (2018). *Categories we live by: The construction of sex, gender, race, and other social categories*. Oxford: Oxford University Press.

Austin, J. L. (1975). *How to do things with words*. Oxford: Oxford University Press.

Ayers, M. R. (1981). Locke versus Aristotle on natural kinds. *The Journal of Philosophy, 78*(5), 247–272.

Bach, T. (2012). Gender is a natural kind with a historical essence. *Ethics, 122*(2), 231–272.

Bach, T. (2016). Social categories are natural kinds, not objective types (and why it matters politically). *Journal of Social Ontology, 2*(2), 177–201.

Beatty, J. (2006). Replaying life's tape. *Journal of Philosophy, 103*, 336–362.

Bem, S. L. (1993). *The lenses of gender: Transforming the debate on sexual inequality*. New Haven, CT: Yale University Press.

Blackless, M., Charuvastra, A., Derryck, A., Fausto-Sterling, A., Lauzanne, K., & Lee, E. (2000). How sexually dimorphic are we? Review and synthesis. *American Journal of Human Biology: The Official Journal of the Human Biology Association, 12*(2), 151–166.

Block, N. (1997). Anti-reductionism slaps back. *Philosophical Perspectives, 11*, 107–132.

Boyd, R. (1991). Realism, anti-foundationalism and the enthusiasm for natural kinds. *Philosophical Studies, 61*(1), 127–148.

Boyd, R. (1999). Kinds, complexity and multiple realization. *Philosophical Studies, 95*, 67–98.

Boyd, R. (2010). Realism, natural kinds, and philosophical methods. In H. Beebee & N. Sabbarton-Leary (Eds.), *The semantics and metaphysics of natural kinds* (pp. 212–234). New York: Routledge.

Broberg, G., & Roll-Hansen, N. (2005). *Eugenics and the welfare state: Norway, Sweden, Denmark, and Finland.* East Lansing, MI: Michigan State University Press.

Bromberger, S. (1997). Natural kinds and questions. *Poznan Studies in the Philosophy of the Sciences and the Humanities, 51,* 149–163.

Brownstein, M. (2019). Implicit bias. In E. N. Zalta (Ed.), *The Stanford encyclopedia of philosophy* (Fall 2019 ed.). Retrieved from https://plato.stanford.edu/archives/fall2019/entries/implicit-bias/.

Brubaker, R. (2004). *Ethnicity without groups.* Cambridge, MA: Harvard University Press.

Buchanan, A., Brock, D. W., Daniels, N., & Wikler, D. (2001). *From chance to choice: Genetics and justice.* Cambridge: Cambridge University Press.

Cantwell, C. (2010). *Buddhism: The basics.* New York: Routledge.

Carens, J. H. (2013). *The ethics of immigration.* Oxford: Oxford University Press.

Cartwright, N. (2009). *The dappled world: A study of the boundaries of science.* Cambridge: Cambridge University Press.

Castro, L., Castro-Nogueira, L., Castro-Nogueira, M. A., & Toro, M. A. (2010). Cultural transmission and social control of human behavior. *Biology & Philosophy, 25*(3), 347–360.

Chevallier, C., Kohls, G., Troiani, V., Brodkin, E. S., & Schultz, R. T. (2012). The social motivation theory of autism. *Trends in Cognitive Sciences, 16*(4), 231–239.

Couch, M. (2005). Functional properties and convergence in biology. *Philosophy of Science, 72*(5), 104–151.

Dembroff, R. (2020). Beyond binary: Genderqueer as critical gender kind. *Philosopher's Imprint, 20*(9), 1–23.

Dennett, D. C. (1991). Real patterns. *The Journal of Philosophy, 88*(1), 27–51.

Desjardins, E. (2011). Historicity and experimental evolution. *Biology and Philosophy, 26,* 339–364.

Devitt, M. (2008). Resurrecting biological essentialism. *Philosophy of Science, 75*(3), 344–382.

Devitt, M. (2010). Species have (partly) intrinsic essences. *Philosophy of Science, 77*(5), 648–661.

Devitt, M. (2018). Historical biological essentialism. *Studies in History and Philosophy of Biological and Biomedical Sciences, 71,* 1–7.

Dias, B. G., & Ressler, K. J. (2014). Parental olfactory experience influences behavior and neural structure in subsequent generations. *Nature Neuroscience, 17*(1), 89–96.

Doolittle, F. W. (1999). Phylogenetic classification and the universal tree. *Science, 284*(5423), 2124–2128.

Dupré, J. (1995). *The disorder of things: Metaphysical foundations of the disunity of science.* Cambridge, MA: Harvard University Press.

Dweck, C. S., Chiu, C., & Hong, Y. (1995). Implicit theories and their role in judgments and reactions: A word from two perspectives. *Psychological Inquiry, 6*(4), 267–285.

Eagly, A., & Wood, W. (2005). Universal sex differences across patriarchal cultures evolved psychological dispositions. *Behavioral and Brain Sciences, 28*(2), 281–283.

Eldridge, M. D. B., Meek, P. D., & Johnson, R. N. (2014). Taxonomic uncertainty and the loss of biodiversity on Christmas Island, Indian Ocean. *Conservation Biology, 28*(2), 572–579.

Epstein, B. (2018). Social ontology. In E. N. Zalta (Ed.), *The Stanford encyclopedia of philosophy* (Summer 2018 ed.). Retrieved from https://plato.stanford.edu/archives/sum2018/entries/social-ontology/

Ereshefsky, M. (2012). Homology thinking. *Biology & Philosophy, 27*(3), 381–400.

Ereshefsky, M. (2014). Species, historicity, and path dependency. *Philosophy of Science, 81*(5), 714–726.

Fodor, J. (1974). Special sciences: Or the disunity of science as a working hypothesis. *Synthese, 28*, 77–115.

Fodor, J. (1997). Special sciences: Still autonomous after all these years. *Philosophical Perspectives, 11*, 149–164.

Fracchia, J., & Lewontin, R. C. (2005). The price of metaphor. *History and Theory, 44*(1), 14–29.

Fricker, M. (2007). *Epistemic injustice: Power and the ethics of knowing*. Oxford: Oxford University Press.

Friedman, J. (2006). Comment on Searle's "social ontology": The reality of the imaginary and the cunning of the non-intentional. *Anthropological Theory, 6*(1), 70–80.

Gannett, L. (2010). Questions asked and unasked: How by worrying less about the "really real" philosophers of science might better contribute to debates about genetics and race. *Synthese, 177*(3), 363–385.

Gelman, S. A. (2004). Psychological essentialism in children. *Trends in Cognitive Sciences, 8*(9), 404–409.

Gendler, T. S. (2011). On the epistemic costs of implicit bias. *Philosophical Studies, 156*(1), 33–53.

Gessen, M. (2018). To be or not to be, *New York Review of Books, 65*(2). Retrieved from https://www.nybooks.com/articles/2018/02/08/to-be-or-not-to-be/.

Gilbert, M. (2013). *On social facts*. Princeton, NJ: Princeton University Press.

Godfrey-Smith, P. (2009). *Darwinian populations and natural selection*. Oxford: Oxford University Press.

Godman, M. (2013). Why we do things together: The social motivation for joint action. *Philosophical Psychology, 26*(4), 588–603.

Godman, M. (2015). The special science dilemma and how culture solves it. *Australasian Journal of Philosophy, 93*(3), 491–508.

Godman, M. (2016a). Möjliga träskindividers omöjliga medlemskap. In I. Niiniluoto, T. Tahko, & T. Toppinen (Eds.), *Mahdollisuus/Möjlighet. Helsingfors: Filosofiska Föreningen i Finland* (pp. 87–93).

Godman, M. (2016b). Cultural syndromes: Socially learned but real. *Filosofia Unisinos, 17*(2), 185–191.

Godman, M. (2018a). Scientific realism with historical essences: The case of species. *Synthese.* https://doi.org/10.1007/s11229-018-02034-3

Godman, M. (2018b). Gender as a historical kind: A tale of two genders? *Biology and Philosophy, 33*(3–4), 21.

Godman, M. (2019). A modern synthesis of philosophy and biology. In K. Becker & I. Thomson (Eds.), *History of philosophy, 1945 to 2015* (pp. 210–220). Cambridge: Cambridge University Press.

Godman, M., Mallozzi, A., & Papineau, D. (2020). Essential properties are super-explanatory: Taming metaphysical modality. *Journal of the American Philosophical Association,* 6(3), 316–334.

Godman, M., Nagatsu, M., & Salmela, M. (2014). The social motivation hypothesis for prosocial behavior. *Philosophy of the Social Sciences*, 44(5), 563–587.

Godman, M., & Papineau, D. (2020). Species have historical not intrinsic essences. In A. Bianchi (Ed.), *Language and reality from a naturalistic perspective: Themes from Michael Devitt*. Philosophical Studies 143, (pp. 355-367). Springer Press.

Gould, S. J. (1986). Evolution and the triumph of homology, or why history matters. *American Scientist, 74*(1), 60–69.

Gould, S. J., & Lewontin, R. C. (1979). The spandrels of San Marco and the Panglossian paradigm: A critique of the adaptationist program. *Proceedings of the Royal Society of London B: Biological Sciences, 205*(1161), 581–598.

Griffiths, P. E. (1999). Squaring the circle: Natural kinds with historical essences. In R. Wilson (Ed.), *Species: New interdisciplinary essays* (pp. 209–228). Cambridge MA: MIT Press.

Guala, F. (2016). *Understanding institutions: The science and philosophy of living together*. Princeton, NJ: Princeton University Press.

Hacking, I. (1991). A tradition of natural kinds. *Philosophical Studies, 61*(1), 109–126.

Hacking, I. (1995). The looping effects of human kinds. In D. Sperber & A. Premack (Eds.), *Causal cognition* (pp. 351–394). Oxford: Clarendon Press.

Hacking, I. (1998). *Mad travelers: Reflections on the reality of transient mental illnesses*. Charlottesville, VA: University of Virginia Press.

Hacking, I. (2007a). Kinds of people: Moving targets. *Proceedings of the British Academy, 151*, 285–318.

Hacking, I. (2007b). Natural kinds: Rosy dawn, scholastic twilight. *Royal Institute of Philosophy Supplements, 61*, 203–239.

Hagerman, M. (2015). *Käraste Herman: Rasbiologen Herman Lundborgs gåta*. Stockholm: Norstedts.

Hagerman, M. (2017). Rasbiologin och forskningsperspektiven: Genmäle till Andreaz Wasniowski. *Historisk Tidskrift (S)*, 137(3), 485–495.

Häggqvist, S. (2005). Kinds, projectibility and explanation. *Croatian Journal of Philosophy, 13*(5), 71–87.

Häggqvist, S., & Wikforss, Å. (2018). Natural kinds and natural kind terms: Myth and reality. *The British Journal for the Philosophy of Science, 69*(4), 911–933.

Haslam, N., Rothschild, L., & Ernst, D. (2002). Are essentialist beliefs associated with prejudice? *British Journal of Social Psychology, 41*(1), 87–100.

Haslanger, S. (2000). Gender and race: (What) are they? (What) do we want them to be? *Noûs, 34*(1), 31–55.

Haslanger, S. (2012). *Resisting reality: Social construction and social critique*. Oxford: Oxford University Press.

Hendry, R. (2016). Natural kinds in chemistry. In G. Fisher & E. Scerri (Eds.), *Essays in the philosophy of chemistry* (pp. 253–275). Oxford: Oxford University Press.

Henrich, J., & McElreath, R. (2003). The evolution of cultural evolution. *Evolutionary Anthropology, 12*, 123–135.

Heyes, C. (2012). What's social about social learning? *Journal of Comparative Psychology, 126*, 193–202.

Hietala, M. (2005). From race hygiene to sterilization: The eugenics movement in Finland. In G. Broberg & N. Roll-Hansen (Eds.), *Eugenics and the welfare state: Norway, Sweden, Denmark, and Finland* (pp. 214–277). East Lansing, MI: Michigan State University Press.

Hindriks, F., & Guala, F. (2015). Institutions, rules, and equilibria: A unified theory. *Journal of Institutional Economics, 11*(3), 459–480.

Hogg, M., & Turner, J. (1985). Interpersonal attraction, social identification and psychological group formation. *European Journal of Social Psychology, 15*(1), 51–66.

Holden, C. J. (2002). Bantu language trees reflect the spread of farming across sub-Saharan Africa: A maximum-parsimony analysis. *Proceedings of the Royal Society of London. Series B: Biological Sciences, 269*(1493), 793–799.

Hong, Y. Y., Coleman, J., Chan, G., Wong, R. Y., Chiu, C. Y., Hansen, I. G., . . . & Fu, H. Y. (2004). Predicting intergroup bias: The interactive effects of implicit theory and social identity. *Personality and Social Psychology Bulletin, 30*(8), 1035–1047.

Horner, V., & Whiten, A. (2005). Causal knowledge and imitation/emulation switching in chimpanzees (Pan troglodytes) and children (Homo sapiens). *Animal Cognition, 8*(3), 164–181.

Hull, D. L. (1975). Central subjects and historical narratives. *History and Theory*, 253–274.

Hull, D. L. (1978). A matter of individuality. *Philosophy of Science, 45*(3), 335–360.

Jablonka, E., & Raz, G. (2009). Transgenerational epigenetic inheritance: Prevalence, mechanisms, and implications for the study of heredity and evolution. *The Quarterly Review of Biology, 84*(2), 131–176.

Johnson, L. M., Matthews, T. L., & Napper, S. L. (2016). Sexual orientation and sexual assault victimization among US college students. *The Social Science Journal, 53*(2), 174–183.

Keller, J. (2005). In genes we trust: The biological component of psychological essentialism and its relationship to mechanisms of motivated social cognition. *Journal of Personality and Social Psychology, 88*(4), 686.

Khalidi, M. A. (2009). Interactive kinds. *The British Journal for the Philosophy of Science, 61*(2), 335–360.

Khalidi, M. A. (2013). *Natural categories and human kinds: Classification in the natural and social sciences*. New York: Cambridge University Press.

Khalidi, M. A. (2018). Natural kinds as nodes in causal networks. *Synthese, 195*(4), 1379–1396.

Kim, J. (1992). Multiple realizability and the metaphysics of reduction. *Philosophy and Phenomenological Research, 52*, 1–26.

Kincaid, H. (2016). Debating the reality of social classes. *Philosophy of the Social Sciences, 46*(2), 189–209.

Kitcher, P. (1984). 1953 and all that. A tale of two sciences. *The Philosophical Review, 93*(3), 335–373.

Kitcher, P. (2007). Does "race" have a future? *Philosophy & Public Affairs, 35*(4), 293–317.

Kornblith, H. (1995). *Inductive inference and its natural ground: An essay in naturalistic epistemology.* Cambridge, MA: MIT Press.

Kripke, S. (1980). *Naming and necessity.* Cambridge, MA: Harvard University Press.

Kung, J. (1977). Aristotle on essence and explanation. *Philosophical Studies, 31*(6), 361–383.

Kunst, J. R., Thomsen, L., & Dovidio, J. F. (2019). Divided loyalties: Perceptions of disloyalty underpin bias toward dually-identified minority-group members. *Journal of Personality and Social Psychology, 117*(4), 807.

Kuorikoski, J., & Pöyhönen, S. (2012). Looping kinds and social mechanisms. *Sociological Theory, 30*(3), 187–205.

Kymlicka, W. (1998). *Mångkulturellt medborgarskap.* Nora, Sweden: Bokförlaget Nya Doxa.

Labba, E. A. (2020). *Herrarna satte oss dit*: Om tvångsförflyttningarna i Sverige. Stockholm: Nordstedts.

Laimann, J. (2020) Capricious Kinds. *The British Journal for the Philosophy of Science, 71*(3), 1043–1068.

LaPorte, J. (2017). Modern essentialism and its animadversions. In R. Joyce (Ed.), *The Routledge handbook of evolution and philosophy* (pp. 182–193). Abingdon: Routledge Press.

Le Guin, U. K. (2012). *The left hand of darkness.* London: Hachette UK.

Lemiere, O. (2018). No purely epistemic theory can account for the naturalness of kinds. *Synthese*, 1–19.

Leslie, S. J. (2008). Generics: Cognition and acquisition. *Philosophical Review, 117*(1), 1–47.

Lewens, T. (2012). Species, essence and explanation. *Studies in History and Philosophy of Science Part C: Studies in History and Philosophy of Biological and Biomedical Sciences, 43*(4), 751–757.

Lewens, T. (2015). *Cultural evolution: Conceptual challenges.* Oxford: Oxford University Press.

Liben, L. S., & Bigler, R. S. (2017). Understanding and undermining the development of gender dichotomies: The legacy of Sandra Lipsitz Bem. *Sex Roles, 76*(9–10), 544–555.

Lim, D. (2014). Is membership always social? *Res Publica, 20*(4), 447–451.

Lippert-Rasmussen, K. (2020). *Making sense of affirmative action.* New York: Oxford University Press.

Lloyd, E. A. (2015). Adaptationism and the logic of research questions: How to think clearly about evolutionary causes. *Biological Theory, 10*(4), 343–362.

Ludwig, D. (2018). Letting go of "natural kind": Toward a multidimensional framework of nonarbitrary classification. *Philosophy of Science, 85*(1), 31–52.

Magnus, P. D. (2012). *Scientific enquiry and natural kinds*. New York: Palgrave Macmillan UK.

Mäkelä, P., & Ylikoski, P. (2003). Others will do it: Social reality by opportunists. In M. Sintonen, P. Ylikoski & K. Miller (Eds.), *Realism in action: Essays in philosophy of the social sciences* (pp. 259–268). Dordrecht: Kluwer Academic.

Mallon, R. (2016). *The construction of human kinds*. Oxford: Oxford University Press.

Mallozzi, A. (2018). Two notions of metaphysical modality. *Synthese*, 1–22.

Mameli, M. (2004). Nongenetic selection and nongenetic inheritance. *The British Journal for the Philosophy of Science*, *55*(1), 35–71.

Mandler, J. M., & McDonough, L. (1998). On developing a knowledge base in infancy. *Developmental Psychology*, *34*(6), 1274.

Matthen, M. (2012). Millikan's historical kinds. In D. Ryder, J. Kingsbury, & K. Willford (Eds.), *Millikan and her critics* (pp. 135–154). Oxford and Malden, MA: Wiley-Blackwell.

Mayr, E. (1961). Cause and effect in biology. *Science*, *134*(3489), 1501–150.

McGuigan, N., Makinson, J., & Whiten, A. (2011). From over imitation to super copying: Adults imitate causally irrelevant aspects of tool use with higher fidelity than young children. *British Journal of Psychology*, *102*(1), 1–18.

Mikkola, M. (2009). Gender concepts and intuitions. *Canadian Journal of Philosophy*, *39*, 559–583.

Mill, J. S. ([1886]1974). *A system of logic, ratiocinative and inductive: Being a connected view of the principles of evidence and the methods of scientific investigation*. Toronto: University of Toronto Press.

Miller, D. (1993). In defense of nationality. *Journal of Applied Philosophy*, *10*(1), 3–16.

Millikan, R. G. (1984). *Language, thought, and other biological categories: New foundations for realism*. Cambridge, MA: MIT Press.

Millikan, R. G. (1998). A common structure for concepts of individuals, stuffs, and real kinds: More Mama, more milk, and more mouse. *Behavioral and Brain Sciences*, *21*(1), 55–65.

Millikan, R. G. (1999). Historical Kinds and the Special Sciences. *Philosophical Studies*, *95*, 45–65.

Millikan, R. G. (2000). *On clear and confused ideas, an essay about substance concepts*. Cambridge: Cambridge University Press.

Millikan, R. G. (2017). *Beyond concepts: Unicepts, language, and natural information*. Oxford: Oxford University Press.

Nanda, S. (1990). *Neither man nor woman: The hijras of India,* Belmont: Wadsworth Publishing.

Nielsen, M., & Blank, C. (2011). Imitation in young children: When who gets copied is more important than what gets copied. *Developmental Psychology*, *47*(4), 1050.

Nielsen, M., & Tomaselli, K. (2010). Overimitation in Kalahari Bushman children and the origins of human cultural cognition. *Psychological Science*, *21*(5), 729–736.

Okasha, S. (2002). Darwinian metaphysics: Species and the question of essentialism. *Synthese*, *131*(2), 191–213.

Papineau, D. (2009). Physicalism and the human sciences. In C. Mantzavinos (Ed.), *Philosophy of the social sciences: Philosophical theory and scientific practice* (pp. 103–123). Cambridge: Cambridge University Press.

Papineau, D. (2010). Can any sciences be special? In C. Macdonald & G. Macdonald (Eds.), *Emergence in mind* (pp. 179–197). New York: Oxford University Press.

Pehrson, S., Brown, R., & Zagefka, H. (2009). When does national identification lead to the rejection of immigrants? Cross-sectional and longitudinal evidence for the role of essentialist in-group definitions. *British Journal of Social Psychology, 48*(1), 61–76.

Pogge, T. W. (1997). Group rights and ethnicity. In I. Shapiro & W. Kymlicka (Eds.), *Ethnicity and group rights: Nomos XXXIX.* New York: NYU Press.

Polger, T. W., & Shapiro, L. A. (2016). *The multiple realization book.* Oxford: Oxford University Press.

Putnam, H. (1975). The meaning of "meaning". In *Philosophical papers: Volume 2, mind, language and reality* (pp. 215–272). Cambridge: Cambridge University Press.

Reydon, T. A. C. (2009). How to fix kind membership: A problem for HPC theory and a solution. *Philosophy of Science, 76*(5), 724–736.

Richerson, P. J., & Boyd, R. (2005). *Not by genes alone: How culture transformed human evolution.* Chicago, IL: University of Chicago Press.

Risse, M. (2016). On the significance of membership in approaches to global justice: Putting Carens in context. *Journal of Applied Philosophy, 33*(4), 443–449.

Ritchie, K. (2015). The metaphysics of social groups. *Philosophy Compass, 10*(5), 310–321.

Roscoe, W. (1991). *The Zuni man-woman.* Albuquerque, NM: University of New Mexico Press.

Salmon, W. C. (1984). *Scientific explanation and the causal structure of the world.* Princeton, NJ: Princeton University Press.

Sánchez-Cuenca, I. (2007). A behavioural critique of Searle's theory of institutions. In S.L Tsohatzidis (Ed.) *Intentional acts and institutional facts: Essays on John Searle's social ontology* (pp. 175–189). Dordrecht: Springer.

Scheff, T. J. (1984). *Being mentally ill* (2nd ed.). Piscataway, NJ: Aldine Transaction.

Searle, J. R. (1969). *Speech acts: An essay in the philosophy of language* (Vol. 626). Cambridge: Cambridge University Press.

Searle, J. R. (2006). Reality and social construction reply to Friedman. *Anthropological Theory, 6*(1), 81–88.

Searle, J. R. (2010). *Making the social world: The structure of human civilization.* Oxford: Oxford University Press.

Shelby, T. (2007). Justice, deviance, and the dark ghetto. *Philosophy & Public Affairs, 35*(2), 126–160.

Slater, M. (2015). Natural kindness. *British Journal for the Philosophy of Science, 66*(2), 375–411.

Sober, E. (2015). *Ockham's razors.* Cambridge: Cambridge University Press.

Spelman, E. (1988). *Inessential woman: Problems of exclusion in feminist thought.* Boston, MA: Beacon Press.

Sterelny, K. (2006). The evolution and evolvability of culture. *Mind and Language, 21*, 137–165.

Sveinsdóttir, Á. K. (2013). The social construction of human kinds. *Hypatia, 28*(4), 716–732.

Tajfel, H. (1981). *Human groups and social categories: Studies in social psychology*. Cambridge: Cambridge University Press.

Tëmkin, I., & Eldredge, N. (2007). Phylogenetics and material cultural evolution. *Current Anthropology, 48*(1), 146–154.

Thomasson, A. L. (2003). Foundations for a social ontology. *ProtoSociology, 18*, 269–290.

Travers, E., Fairhurst, M. T., & Deroy, O. (2020). Racial bias in face perception is sensitive to instructions but not introspection. *Consciousness and Cognition, 83*, 102952.

Tuomela, R. (2010). *The philosophy of sociality: The shared point of view*. Oxford: Oxford University Press.

Užgiris, I. (1981). Two functions of imitation during infancy. *International Journal of Behavioral Development, 4*(1), 1–12.

Valkonen, J., Valkonen, S., & Koivurova, T. (2016). Groupism and the politics of indigeneity: A case study on the Sámi debate in Finland. *Ethnicities*, 1468796816654175.

Walzer, M. (1983). *Spheres of justice: A defense of pluralism and equality*. New York: Basic Books.

Wasniowski, A. (2017a). Maja Hagerman, Käraste Herman: Rasbiologen Herman Lundborgs gåta. *Historisk Tidskrift (S), 137*(1), 162–165.

Wasniowski, A. (2017b). Replik på Maja Hagermans genmäle. *Historisk Tidskrift (S), 137*(3), 496–501.

Weisberg, M., Needham, P., & Hendry, R. (2019). Philosophy of chemistry. In *The Stanford encyclopedia of philosophy*. (Spring 2019 Edition), Edward N. Zalta (ed.), URL = <https://plato.stanford.edu/archives/spr2019/entries/chemistry/>.

Weiskopf, D. A. (2011). The functional unity of special science kinds. *British Journal for the Philosophy of Science, 62*(2), 233–258.

Wood, W., & Eagly, A. H. (2012). Biosocial construction of sex differences and similarities in behavior. *Advances in Experimental Social Psychology, 46*(1), 55–123.

Wood, W. & Eagly, A. (2015). Two traditions of research on gender identity. *Sex Roles, 73*(11), 461–473.

Wood, W., Eagly, A., & Eisenberg, N. (2002). A cross-cultural analysis of the behavior of women and men: Implications for the origins of sex differences. *Psychological Bulletin, 128*(5), 699–727.

Yehuda, R., Daskalakis, N. P., Bierer, L. M., Bader, H. N., Klengel, T., Holsboer, F., & Binder, E. B. (2016). Holocaust exposure induced intergenerational effects on FKBP5 methylation. *Biological Psychiatry, 80*(5), 372–380.

Young, I. M. (1994). Gender as seriality: Thinking about women as a social collective. *Signs, 19*(3), 713–738.

Zack, N. (2014). The philosophical roots of racism and its legacy. Confluence, 1, 85–98.

# Index

Abrahamic religion 71, 73
affirmative action 89, 96n10
Alexievich, Svetlana 78
anthropology 54, 74–75; *see also* physical anthropology
anti-essentialism 12–13
Armenians 78–79
astronomical kinds 10
autism 37
Azerbaijani 78–79

Bach, Theodore 18, 46, 59, 65–67
Baku pogrom 78
baseball batters 30–31
Bem, Sandra 59
Block, Ned 23–24
Boyd, Richard 34–36, 51
Boyd, Robert 74, 86
Brubaker, Roger 91
Buddhism 73–76, 79

Cantwell, Cathy 73
Carens, Josef 90
case study: approach 3, 97; concept of 6
cats 70–71
causal nodes 35–36
chemical kinds 10, 47, 49, 56n6
Christianity 49, 71
Christmas Island shrew (*Crocidura attenuata trichura*) 53
class 66, 80, 95n2
clones 53
collective recognition 28–34; identity of collective 32–34
common cause explanations 10–13, 16–18; applied to kinds 12–13; *vs.* explanations of single

generalizations 16–17; as levers for change 16–18; *see also* lineages, as common cause explanations; proximate explanations, *vs.* common cause explanations; ultimate explanations, *vs.* common cause explanations
comparative tendency 6–7, 15, 35, 72
compulsive wandering 38–39
conformity 37, 40–43, 60–61, 85–87; biases 86
conservation 53
content biases 86
convergent evolution 25, 53, 65–68, 84; in culture 65–68, 84
Couch, Mark 25–26
cross-cultural psychology 64–65
cultural evolution 2, 61, 74, 76–77, 85–88, 96n6
cultural kinds 58–77, 81–88, 92–95, 98–99; inferential principals of 67–68, 70–75; *vs.* kinds of people 70; multiple realization of 75–77
cultural selection 24–26, 66–68, 85
culture 2, 24, 45, 54, 58–77, 81–88, 92–95, 98–99

Dadas, Albert 38–39
Darwin, Charles 52
declarations 28–30
deontic powers *see* status functions
developmental psychology 14–15, 60, 71, 87–88
Devitt, Michael 48–49, 54, 56n6, 57n11
discrimination 14, 79, 89–90
DNA methylation 86
doctors 6–7, 29–30, 44n8

domain-specificity 21–22, 36, 91, 97;
  *see also* pluralism
Dweck, Carol 40–41

Eagly, Alice 60, 63
economic categories 64, 95n2
eliminativism 80, 91; *see also* pluralism
epigenetics 50, 60, 85–86; *see also*
  reproduction, mechanisms of; social
  learning
Ereshefsky, Marc 49–50, 54–55
essentialism 11–15, 17, 19n11, 19n14,
  54; historical essentialism 11;
  intrinsic essentialism 57n11; nominal
  essences 19n13; origin essentialism
  54–55; psychological essentialism
  14–15, 17
ethnicity 78–88; as a historical kind
  78–83; language markers of 81–82;
  status transformation of 83–89
eugenics 15, 80–84; positive 84
evolutionary biology 48–49, 74
experimentation 6
eye 25–26

Finns 80–84
Fodor, Jerry 5, 22–24
functional kinds *see* convergent
  evolution; human kinds, as
  functional kinds

game theory 31–32
gay, as a kind 31–32
gender 6–7, 17, 18–19n4, 29, 38, 41,
  58–69; as a cross-cultural kind
  64–68; cultural reproduction of
  58–61; cultural variation of 58,
  61–64; *vs.* sex 59–63, 69n3; variation
  over time 61
gender identity research 60
genderqueer 69n6
generalizations 5–11, 15–18; *ceteris
  paribus* 5, 23; examples of in the
  human sciences 6; *vs.* institutional
  facts 27, 29–31; justifications for
  in the human sciences 6–8, 15–17;
  lawful 5–6; scope of 6, 53, 68, 74–75;
  selection-based 24–26; universal 5–6;
  *see also* comparative tendency
generics 7
Godfrey-Smith, Peter 46–47

Gould, Stephen J. 52, 66–67
group rights 89–95; *vs.* individual
  rights 92
Guala, Francesco 17, 31–32

Hacking, Ian 34
Haslanger, Sally 16, 93
higher kinds 70–75; templates for
  71–76
higher taxa 9–10, 71
*hijra* 62
historical explanations *see* lineages, as
  common cause explanations; path-
  dependency; ultimate explanations
historical injustice 89, 91, 94
historical kinds 1–4, 45–100; boundaries
  between 54–55; *vs.* eternal kinds 49,
  56n6; as higher kinds 70–75; models
  *see* models (of historical kinds); time-
  slices of 70, 75–76, 92
homeostasis *see* human kinds, as
  homeostatic property clusters
horse (*Equus ferus*) 8–13, 19n9, 42; *vs.*
  white horse 8–10, 36, 45–46, 52
human kinds: epistemology of 5–13,
  48–57, 61–77; as functional kinds
  25–26, 30, 44n6, 64–66, 97, 99;
  as historical kinds 45–100; as
  homeostatic property clusters 34–36,
  43; as levers for change 15–18;
  morality of 13–18, 78–96; moral
  valence of 37–40, 78–80, 83–85,
  89; as moving targets 37–40, 43,
  84; and the natural kind tradition
  8–13, 34, 99; scope of 3, 97; as
  social constructions 40–45; as
  social institutions 27–34; status
  transformations of 78–89; as
  teleofunctional kinds 65–68
human sciences 5–10, 15–16, 18,
  71–73, 77; definition of 5

identity (social) 60–61
identity politics 94–95
imitation *see* overimitation; social
  learning
implicit bias 14, 20n15
indigenous groups 83, 89, 94, 96n5
injustice: detection of 15–16; *see also*
  historical injustice; human kinds, as
  levers for change; structural injustice

institutional facts 28–31; *vs.* discovered
    fallouts 30–31; *vs.* empirical
    generalizations 27
interdisciplinarity 77
Internet 11, 76

Khalidi, Muhammad 35–36, 38, 47
Kim, Jaegwon 23
kinds 4n2, 8–13; concepts of 4n1,
    18n1; open-ended 8–9; *vs.* properties
    8; *see also* human kinds
kinds of people *see* cultural kinds, *vs.*
    kinds of people
Kitcher, Philip 48–49
Kymlicka, Will 90, 96n12

labeling effects 37, 87
lateral transmission *see* reproduction,
    lateral
Le Guin, Ursula 62
Leslie, Sara-Jane 7
Lewontin, Richard 66–67, 85
lineages: as common-cause
    explanations 48–51; counterfactual
    force of 50; as demarcating
    kinds 51–57, 61–68, 72–75, 91;
    requirements for 47; solidarity
    between 67–68; solidarity within
    94; reconstruction of 53–54;
    *vs.* timelines 50; *see also* path-
    dependency; reproduction
Lloyd, Elisabeth 66
Locke, John 12, 19n13
looping effects *see* human kinds, as
    moving targets
Lundborg, Herman 81–84

mad travelling *see* compulsive wandering
Mallozzi, Antonella 19n11
Mayr, Ernst 48, 52
mercury 70
Mill, John Stuart 8–9, 19n10
Millikan, Ruth 2, 4n1, 8, 10, 18n1,
    46–47, 49, 64–65, 70–73
minority rights *see* group rights
models (of historical kinds) 46–47,
    50–51, 58–64, 78; origins of 49,
    55–56; ritualization of 63
models (theoretical) 26
multiple projectability 8–13; and
    multiple realization 25–27, 75–77;

non-accidentality of 10–11; and
    open-ended enquiry 8–9; trade-off
    with scope of application 74–75
multiple realization 22–27, 75–77;
    trade-off with multiple projectability
    25–27; via selected function 24–27
mutations 50, 54

nationalism 82–84
natural kinds *see* kinds
niche 38–41, 60–61, 86–87
niche construction 50; cultural 86–87
non-genetic inheritance *see* epigenetics

oral tradition 75–76, 77n4
overimitation 87–88

pain 22, 24–25
Papineau, David 23–26
path-dependency 49–50, 54–55
personal identity 92
phylogenetics 53–54; in the human
    sciences 54, 74
physical anthropology 80–84;
    ideological elements of 80, 82–84
physicalism 21–22
pluralism: about human kinds 36; about
    social membership 91;
    *see also* domain-specificity
political philosophy and theory 89–96
power relations 32–34, 79, 83–85; as
    causing selection 85
primates 74
projectability, dilemma of 23;
    *see also* generalizations; multiple
    projectability
prokaryotes 72
proximate explanations 17, 41–43,
    48–49; *vs.* common cause
    explanations 48–49; *vs.* ultimate
    explanations 48
psychological essentialism *see*
    essentialism, psychological
    essentialism

race 10, 15, 32, 41–42, 79–84, 88,
    96n3; cladistic account of 96n4;
    cultural reproduction *vs.* biological
    reproduction 82–83; as ethnicity
    81–83; in the Nordic early 20th
    century 80–81

racial segregation 41–42
racism 83–84
reductionism 21–23
religion 71, 73–77, 79, 94, 98
repatriation 89
reproduction: conditions for 47; lateral 56n2, 68, 72; *vs.* mass production 47; mechanisms of 47, 50, 58–61, 75–76, 85–88; *see also* lineages
Retzius, Anders 80
Richerson, Peter 74, 86
role model 86, 88
Roscoe, Will 62–63

Salmon, Wesley 11
Sámi: as an ethnicity 82–83, 84; forced Christian schooling of 83; forcible relocation of 83; looping effects of 84; physical anthropology of 80–83; psychological scars of 84–88, 93–95; sense of inferiority among 84–88; status transformation of 83; supposed homogeneity of 84
science, and value-free enquiry 15, 18; *see also* human sciences
Searle, John 27–34
selected function *see* human kinds, as functional kinds; human kinds, as teleofunctional kinds
sex 59; *see also* gender, *vs.* sex
sexuality (or sexual orientation) 80, 89–90; *see also* gay, as a kind
social approval (and disapproval) 60–61
social categories, representations of 40–43; *see also* kinds, concepts of
social class *see* class
social constructivism 16, 40–43, 99, 100n1; *see also* human kinds, as social constructions
social institutions 27–31
social learning 58–64, 67–68, 75–76, 83, 86–88; aim of 60–61, 87–88; of maladaptive behavior 86–87
social media 68
social membership (in political philosophy and theory) 90–91
social motivations 87–88
social ontology 27, 96n9
social psychology 13–16, 40–41, 59, 60
solidarity 67–68, 92, 94–95, 96n5

Soto Zen Buddhism 74, 76
spandrels 66–67
special sciences 5, 22
species 9, 11, 35–36, 46, 50–55, 71–72; as historical kinds 46, 50–55; reproductive mechanisms of 35–36, 50, 72
speech acts 28–30
Spelman, Elizabeth 58
status functions 29–34, 79
status transformations 79–80, 83–85, 89, 92, 99
Sterelny, Kim 86–87
structural explanations *see* proximate explanations
structural injustice 89, 93–94
student essay example 11, 17, 19n12
subordination 92–95
swamp kinds 52–53
swamp tigers *see* swamp kinds

Tajfel, Henri 13
teleofunctions 65; *see also* human kinds, as teleofunctional kinds
theoretical model 26
third gender 62–63
Thomasson, Amie 32
tigers (*Panthera tigris*) 52
timeline 50
transgender 6
twin earth cases
two-spirit *see* third gender

ultimate explanations 48–49; *vs.* common cause explanations 49; *vs.* proximate explanations 48
Užgiris, Ina 60

vertebrates 71

Walzer, Michael 90
*War and Peace* 46, 49
Weiskopf, Daniel 26
We'wha 62–63
white horse *see* horse (*Equus ferus*), *vs.* white horse
White supremacists 92, 95
Wood, Wendy 60, 63

Young, Iris Marion 90, 91

Zuni tribe 62–63

Printed in the United States
by Baker & Taylor Publisher Services